THE EQUALITY
OF EDUCATIONAL
OPPORTUNITY

A Bibliography of Selected References

THE EQUALITY OF EDUCATIONAL OPPORTUNITY

A Bibliography of Selected References

FRANCESCO CORDASCO
Montclair State College

WITH

MAURIE HILLSON
RUTGERS—THE STATE UNIVERSITY
OF NEW JERSEY

EUGENE BUCCHIONI
CITY UNIVERSITY OF NEW YORK

ROWMAN AND LITTLEFIELD
Totowa, New Jersey

Published 1973 by Littlefield, Adams & Co.

Copyright 1973 by Francesco Cordasco

Library of Congress Cataloging in Publication Data

Cordasco, Francesco, 1920-
The Equality of Educational Opportunity.

1. Educational equalization—United States.
I. Hillson, Maurie, joint author.
II. Bucchioni, Eugene, joint author. III. Title.
LA210.C58   1973   016.37019'34'0973   73-7595
ISBN 0-87471-202-5

Printed in the United States of America

For
MICHAEL
  and
    CARMELA

TABLE OF CONTENTS

PREFACE

The quest for equal educational opportunity in the United States extends back to the very founding of the republic; and it is hardly fortuitous that the American educational historian, Lawrence A. Cremin, subtitled his *The American Common School* "an historic conception."[1]

In a foreword to the Cremin monograph, the social reformer George S. Counts astutely observed "the 'founding fathers' of the common school understood the relation between education and political systems;" and he further perceptively noted: "They [the founding fathers] rejected the idea that education is an autonomous process conducted according to its own laws, welcomed by free societies and feared by despotisms. They accepted as axiomatic the view that there is an appropriate form of education for every society, that the educational practices developed in monarchical states beyond the Atlantic were unsuited and even dangerous to republican America, and that the American people should develop a very special kind of school appropriate to their free institutions and democratic ideas. This profound insight into the nature of education was often lost or obscured in later generations."[2]

The "special kind of school" which Americans developed inevitably resulted in educational opportunity for millions of human beings who, in other periods of time and in other societies, could have expected no educational opportunity at all.[3]

---

[1] Lawrence A. Cremin, *The American Common School: An Historic Conception* (New York: Bureau of Publications, Teachers College, Columbia University, 1951).

[2] *Ibid.*, pp. vii–viii.

[3] Despite the many criticisms leveled agained the American school, there can be little argument with its general success as a vehicle of economic enfranchisement for millions of its students. A salutary correction to many of the ideological assaults against the schools is Harry S. Broudy, *The Real World of the Public Schools* (New York: Harcourt Brace Jovanovich, 1972). But the school's successes were not achieved without exactment of a heavy price: see generally, F. Cordasco, "The Children of Immigrants in the Schools: Historical Analogues of Educational Deprivation," *Kansas Journal of Sociology,* vol. 6 (Fall 1970), pp. 143–152; and with some change, *Journal of Negro Education,* Winter 1973.

But the ideal of the *equality* of educational opportunity in American society has remained elusive. Vast disenfranchised constituencies (the contemporary poor) seem to lie outside the vertiginous socio-economic transformations wrought by the free schools of a free society in other periods in American history; and, as in no other time, the schools have become the battleground of unyielding opportunities sought by the new poor.

That the quest for equality of opportunity (in education and in all else) was and continues real is nowhere more affirmed than in that extraordinary "War on Poverty" largely coterminous with the presidencies of John F. Kennedy (1960–1963) and Lyndon B. Johnson (1963–1968). In a sense, the ebullient optimism of the period ended with the assassination of Robert F. Kennedy in 1968; and the sombre reflection of Daniel P. Moynihan is a grimly poetic epitaph of the seemingly lost and elusive ideal:

> There is, of course, at this moment a sense of an even larger drama having ended. As I write I am just returned from the funeral of Robert F. Kennedy. It was not in any sense a triumph, as in a way his brother's funeral had been a triumph. It was, rather, a long, desolate, remorseless demonstration of defeat. We lost. The momentary generosity of our enemies is compounded primarily of that knowledge. The 'we' includes many people, but to an intensive degree it includes those whose names will appear in this narrative. By and large they had scattered in the ineluctable diaspora that followed the assassination of John F. Kennedy. Now they had gathered to accompany his brother to that slight knoll in Arlington cemetery near the eternal flame that in warning and reproach gleams across Memorial Bridge to the sacred precincts of the city . . .
>
> Not a pantheon perhaps, but a list of men who hoped much for their country, but whose hopes for this moment, at least, seemed to have come to little more than the burial by moonlight of a leader who in the face of setback and disappointment did not lower, but indeed raise, *his* expectations for that country. In a curious sense community action is an idea that came more and more to be associated with Robert F. Kennedy, even as he grew further removed from the centers of power in Washington where (such being the irony of things) its official fate was determined. If there be those who feel there is no power in the idea, they would have done well to ride that funeral train and to watch the poor of America standing vigil as his body passed by. For the moment uncertainty is all, reconciliation distant. Yet in the

gentleness and endurance of those faces there was all the hope
that any nation ought to need, or could expect to have."[4]

The present volume largely derives from the momentum
generated in the 1960s in pursuit of the ideal of the equality of
educational opportunity. Primarily, it is a bibliography of titles
selected from that vast literature spawned in the 1960s (and
extending into the next decade) which deals with the American
schools and the children of the poor: with the so called "minority child" (blacks, Puerto Ricans, Mexican-Americans, Indians,
the "Appalachian poor," ethnics, migrants); with the surging
restiveness of community involvements; the desegregation of
urban schools; with multifarious educational experiments and
failing innovative designs; and with the twin themes of alienation and disaffection. The bibliography's entries have been
arranged under five main categories: Role of the School; Dropouts and Delinquency; Characteristics of the Disadvantaged
Student; Teachers and Teacher Education; and Programs and
Materials. Where appropriate, I have affixed some annotation
to the titles and I have prefaced the register of titles with a
brief bibliographical essay which sketches the socio-economic
and political contexts which make educational history an integral part of the greater societal matrix.[5]

I have also provided a long essay which places into focus the
quest for the equality of educational opportunity, furnishing a
framework into which the basic data have been set and the
historical parameters defined; with the modalities of educational inequality, the early efforts in behalf of the children of
the poor, and the patterns of federal intervention placed into

[4] Daniel P. Moynihan, *Maximum Feasible Misunderstanding: Community Action in the War on Poverty* (New York: Free Press, 1969),
pp. xix–xx.

[5] The bibliography was first published when I was invited by the American Library Association to compile a checklist of titles which dealt with
poor children and schools, *i.e.*, F. Cordasco, "Poor Children and Schools,"
Choice, vol. 7, (April–May 1970), pp. 202–212, 355–356; it was re-
published (with some expansion), F. Cordasco and M. Hillson, "The
School and the Children of the Poor: A Bibliography of Selected References," in W. W. Brickman and S. Lehrer, eds., *Education and the
Many Faces of the Disadvantaged* (New York: John Wiley, 1972), pp.
389–410. It has been greatly expanded for the present volume, and its
400 entries constitute a profile of our age's efforts in behalf of poor children and the extension of educational opportunity. See the bibliographical
essay, *Infra*, for supplemental bibliographical aids.

an intelligible historical design;[6] and I have included a profile
of the travail of the Puerto Rican community as it seeks educational opportunity.[7] No document in the literature of the
American school of this period is more important than the
final *Report* of the Urban Education Task Force, one of a number of task forces convened in March, 1969 by Robert H.
Finch, then Secretary of Health, Education, and Welfare. The
Urban Education Task Force was headed by Dr. Wilson C.
Riles and was assigned by Dr. James E. Allen, Jr. (then Assistant Secretary/Commissioner of Education—designate) a high
priority in seeking solutions for the deepening urban educational crisis. The Task Force completed its *Report* in Novem-
ber/December 1969, and submitted it to Dr. Allen in January,
1970. For whatever the reason, the *Report* was not made public, and only its publication by Rep. Jeffery Cohelan (*D. California*) in the *Congressional Record* (January 19–20, 1970)
brought it to attention.[8] Despite the fact that it remains the
fullest exposition of the urban educational crisis and presents
a detailed plan for the remediation of most of the ills, it has
not been acted upon. I have included the *Summary* of the
Report in this volume, since (in my judgment) it demonstrates

[6] Adapted from F. Cordasco, "America and The Quest for Equal Educational Opportunity: A Prolegomenon and Overview," *British Journal
of Educational Studies*, vol. 21 (February 1973).

[7] Adapted from F. Cordasco, "Introduction," *The Puerto Rican Study,
1953–1957. A Report on the Education and Adjustment of Puerto Rican
Pupils in the Public Schools of the City of New York* (New York: Oriole
Editions, 1972), pp. iii–xxiii.

[8] The complete text of the *Report* is available in *The Urban Education
Task Force Report. Final Report of the Task Force on Urban Education
to the Department of Health, Education, and Welfare*. Wilson C. Riles,
Chairman (New York: Praeger, 1970). "It gives me great pleasure to
write this introduction to the report of President Nixon's Task on Urban
Education on the occasion of its publication in the Praeger Special Studies
series. This report first came to my attention early in January, 1970 when
the entire Congress was deeply involved in the final passage of the education appropriations for fiscal year 1970. During the long and at times
acrimonious debate over this legislation, there was an overriding concern
that the President would veto this bill, to which the Congress had added
$1 billion over the Presidential request. This the President did. The
official reason was "inflation," but to many of us who had led the fight
to fully fund education, the real reason for the veto was the question of
domestic priorities. To the members of Congress who had fought hard to
add these vitally needed educational funds, the Administration's position
was untenable." (From the *Foreword* by Rep. Jeffery Cohelan).

quite clearly our ability to deal with the problems of educational inequality and neglect. The reasons for our disinclination to act may well lie in the byzantine politics which ineluctably surround all social reform.

The gathering of the materials in this volume is intended to serve the needs of many students of American education who seek a convenient guide to the literature of the equality of educational opportunity as it has developed over the last decade. The book should prove useful in courses in urban education; the sociology of education; the proliferating courses in Black studies, and ethnic relations; and in a wide gamut of courses in urban sociology and the new metropolitanism. For libraries, it affords a convenient bibliographical register in a critical area of concern. The interpretative glosses and emphases which I have provided (and, for that matter, the recommendations of the Urban Education Task Force) may not be completely accepted, but, hopefully, will delineate some salient guidelines in the use of the bibliography.

I am indebted to Dr. Maurie Hillson who worked on the early drafts of the bibliography and to Dr. Eugene Bucchioni, colleague and coworker in the *barrios* of American cities; and to a host of other individuals, both within and outside the academic community, with whom I have worked in deteriorating urban contexts. Angela B. Jack, my tireless assistant, shares any credit which inures to this modest *opusculo*.

F. C.

America and the Quest for Equal Educational Opportunity:

The Schools and the Children of the Poor

THE SCHOOLS AND THE CHILDREN
OF THE POOR

I INTRODUCTION

The school, more than any other social agency, provides the
patterns of social mobility. In an American class-less society in
which a long history of commitment to popular education exists,
the schools should have assured not only access to the opportunities of the society, but equally participative roles for all
citizens: meaningful roles which demonstrated that the school
was a basic denominator and index of success for all its children.

The United States of America presents an excellent case study
for analysis and review; and this essay proposes an historical
overview of educational experience in the United States, with
special reference to the patterns of educational inequality, early
efforts in behalf of the children of the poor, and the federal
interventions (both early and recent) in which possible solutions were proposed.[1] American society *is* a class-less society
with a long history of commitment to popular education; but
its schools have not provided equal educational opportunity to
all children. Discrimination against blacks (segregation, separate school systems, etc.) has been part of a pervasive policy

[1] "If the term 'minority child' is used, and the social context is one of
deprivation (whatever form it takes, *viz.*, ghettoization; segregated schools;
cultural assault and enforced change, etc.), the term may be enlarged to
comprehend the urban black in-migrant poor; Puerto Rican migrants to
mainland cities; the Mexican-American poor of the Southwest; the economically displaced white poor (the euphemism is 'Appalachian poor');
reservation Indians and migrant Indians; the ethnic poor who have recently entered because of relaxed immigration quotas; the agricultural
seasonally-employed poor caught in migrancy and rootlessness; and in the
broad historical sense, the ethnic poor of other eras." See F. Cordasco,
"Poor Children and Schools," *Choice* (American Library Association),
vol. 7 (April–May 1970), p. 202.

which discriminated against the poor who included amongst themselves the ethnics (who profiled a long and continuing history of immigration to America); Mexicans, who resisted the efforts at enforced assimilation; and poor whites generally, the victims of socio-economic disadvantage. In a multi-racial, ethnically variegated society, the American experience (certainly, in its schools) has been an experience of cultural assault, discriminatory rejection of educational opportunity for many children, and the continuation of social and economic advantage for a white Anglo-Saxon, Protestant, middle-class patrician elite. It was not until the 1950s that these practices were decisively challenged, and massive efforts (largely government-sponsored) were made to provide better educational opportunity to the poor.

II EDUCATION AND THE PATTERNS OF INEQUALITY

Professor Cremin has observed that the American common [i.e., "popular"] school "emerged as a response to the conditions of American life."

> The American common school emerged as a response to the conditions of American life. Its development during the Middle Period [for purposes of this study, 1815–1850] may be closely related to four basic social and intellectual trends in the early life of the Republic: (1) the democratizing of politics; (2) the growth of the struggle to maintain social equality; (3) the change in the conception of man and society; and (4) the rise of nationalism. Essentially, the common school represented one means by which citizens of that era sought consciously to meet certain of the problems implicit in these board cultural changes.[2]

By 1850, the concept of the "common school" had in "its own right become a genuine part of that life [of the American nation] standing as a principal positive commitment of the American people."[3]

Obviously, the "commitment" differed in different parts of the Union. Before the Civil War, American blacks were generally

---

[2] Lawrence A. Cremin, *The American Common School: An Historic Conception* (New York: Bureau of Publications, Teachers College, Columbia University, 1951), p. 1. See also, Sidney L. Jackson, *America's Struggle for Free Schools* (New York: Russell & Russell, 1965 [orig. 1941]).

[3] Cremin, *op. cit.*, p. 219.

excluded from any educational opportunity;[4] and, following the Civil War, educational facilities for blacks were very inadequate.[5] The separate but equal doctrine which held that it was constitutional to segregate black pupils for purposes of school attendance was affirmed in *Plessey v. Ferguson* (1897; 163 U.S. 537), and was to stand until it was struck down by the U.S. Supreme Court in 1954 (*Brown v. Board of Education*, 347 U.S. 483). Blacks, historically, lay outside (however paradoxical) the common school concept. Despite all the efforts (both private and state) to bring blacks within the conceptual framework that the common school imposed, the resistances encountered made progress both slow and uneven. The exclusion of the blacks was accomplished by what Professor Bullock has called "the great detour:"

It was this great detour that gave special education such a special place in the Negroes' long struggle to gain educational opportunities. Special education was more than a series of public schools and colleges. It was even more than the system of industrial education to which most of the public schools were turning at that time. It was a way of life to which Negroes were exposed for the purpose of perpetuating their caste condition, and the schools were to serve merely as the formal channel of this educative process.

Therefore, it was planned that the maintenance of Southern traditions as related to Negroes would come through a neat biracial arrangement of peoples and expectations. Negroes were to be kept socially isolated from whites by means of a rigid system of residential segregation; they were to be limited to special occupational pursuits by means of job restrictions; they were to be tailored in "Negro ways" through a rigid code of interracial etiquette; and they were to be reinforced in their obedience to caste rules through formal schooling. The point at which this biracial society began forming a way of life for Negroes, tailoring them into a particular social type, and utilizing the schools to serve the ends of segregation marks the real beginning of Negro education as a traditional American institution.[6]

[4] See Carter G. Woodson, *The Education of the Negro Prior to 1861* (New York: G. P. Putnam's Sons, 1915); and Henry A. Bullock, *A History of Negro Education in the South* (Cambridge: Harvard University Press, 1967).

[5] See Edgar W. Knight, *The Influence of Reconstruction on Education in the South* (New York: Bureau of Publications, Teachers College, Columbia University, 1913); and Virgil A. Clift, *et al.*, *Negro Education in America* (New York: Harper, 1962).

[6] Henry A. Bullock, *op. cit.*, pp. 147–148.

The evolving patterns of educational inequality in the American experience extend beyond American blacks. The exclusion of blacks did not resolve the ongoing challenges to the uniformity of American character which in the last decades of the 19th century continued to appear on every side. Immigrants presented special problems to the schools, particularly in industrial-urban contexts. The school saw its role as one which imposed assimilation on the immigrant child. Cubberley, the American educational historian, makes this vividly clear:

> Everywhere these people [immigrants] tend to settle in groups or settlements and to set up their own national manners, customs and observances. Our task is to *break up* their groups and settlements, to assimilate or amalgamate these people as a part of the American race, and to implant in their children, so far as can be done, the Anglo-Saxon conception of righteousness, law, order, and popular government, and to awaken in them reverence for our democratic institutions and for those things which we as people hold to be of abiding worth.[7]

Skeletally framed, American schools rejected black pupils, repudiated the cultural differences of the children of immigrants, and encapsulated within separate spheres other subcommunities (*e.g.*, Mexicans and Indians) which threatened what the American schools envisioned as a homogeneous social order oriented to models which were white, Anglo-Saxon, Protestant, and middle-class. It sorted out the blacks, enforced the assimilation of different social enclaves, and generally ignored the educational needs of intransigent groups. In the process, the American school praticed both racial and ethnic discrimination against the children of the poor.[8]

[7] Ellwood P. Cubberley, *Changing Conceptions of Education* (Boston: Houghton Mifflin, 1909), p. 16. See also, Leonard P. Ayres, *Laggards in our Schools* (New York: Russell Sage Foundation, 1909); and as a point of dissent, Jane Addams, "The Public School and the Immigrant Child," National Education Association *Journal*, vol. 46 (June 1908), pp. 99–102. See also, F. Cordasco, "Introduction," *Report on the Children of Immigrants in Schools* (Metuchen, N.J.: Scarecrow Reprint Corporation, 1970) which is part (vols. 29–33) of the U.S. Immigration Commission: *Report of the Immigration Commission*. 41 vols. (Washington: Government Printing Office, 1911). For immigrant children at the turn of the 19th century, see F. Cordasco, *Jacob Riis Revisited: Poverty and the Slum in Another Era* (New York: Doubleday, 1968).

[8] The patterns of exclusion and/or repudiation can be traced in Robert H. Bremner, ed., *Children and Youth in America: A Documentary History*, vol. I [1600–1865]; vol. II [1866–1932] (Cambridge: Harvard Uni-

III EARLY EFFORTS IN BEHALF OF
THE CHILDREN OF THE POOR

A vast literature exists on poverty in America. It compre-
hends the history of private charitable and philantropic endeavors; the rise of social work; reports and investigations of poverty
under a multiplicity of auspices; and the chronicling of poverty
in both literature and art.[9]

However, American educational historians have, for the most
part, ignored the study of poverty and the schools.[10] It is not
that the sources for the study do not exist; rather, it would
appear that historians have failed to see the school in American
society as committed to cultural ideals related to social class,
life styles, and the perpetuation of an elite. In essence, the
schools were inimical to the very identities that many of the
children brought to the classroom.

In the pervasive poverty of American society, efforts in behalf
of poor children derived from many areas. Voluntary agencies
provided some elementary instruction for the poor, and these
agencies were for the most part extensions of British parent
models or adaptations, e.g., Sunday Schools, the British and
Foreign School Society, and the National Society for Promoting

versity Press, 1970–71). See also, Robert H. Bremner, *From the Depths:
The Discovery of Poverty in the United States* (New York: New York
University Press, 1956); and as a corpus of late 19th century and early
20th century texts, F. Cordasco, ed., *The Social History of Poverty: The
Urban Experience*, 15 vols. (New York: Garrett Press, 1969–1970) which
reprints works by Jane Addams, Charles Loring Brace (a founder of the
Children's Aid Society), Helen Campbell, Edward N. Clopper, Hutchins
Hapgood, Robert Hunter, Jacob A. Riis, John Spargo, Robert A. Woods,
and Carroll Davidson Wright.

[9] See Robert H. Bremner, *From the Depths: The Discovery of Poverty
in the United States* for a kaleidoscopic overview of the sources and
literature.

[10] New interpretations and emphases appear to have emerged. See
Bernard Bailyn, *Education in the Forming of American Society* (Chapel
Hill: University of North Carolina Press, 1960); and Lawrence A. Cremin,
*The Wonderful World of Ellwood P. Cubberley: An Essay on the His-
toriography of American Education* (New York: Bureau of Publications,
Teachers College, Columbia University, 1965). See also a perceptive
essay by Michael B. Katz, "Education and Social Development in the
Nineteenth Century: New Directions for Enquiry," in Paul Nash, ed.,
History and Education: The Educational Uses of the Past (New York:
Random House, 1970), pp. 83–114.

the Education of the Poor.[11] With the secularization of American schools, the wide use of monitorial methods of instruction introduced by Joseph Lancaster (1778–1838) have a special importance.[12] The development of free public schools was impeded by the conception of free schools as pauper schools. The very desperate conditions of the poor (particularly in an industrial-urban America) brought into being a wide range of efforts in behalf of poor children, none more influential and effective than the Children's Aid Society founded in 1853;[13] and between 1870–1920, social reformers, philanthropists, and legislators remained preoccupied with the improvement of the conditions of the poor.[14] Efforts in behalf of American blacks reflected the disorganization of what little public education existed after the Civil War. Although the Peabody Education Fund invigorated the development of education in the South, blacks gained little; and it might be argued that the munificence of the Slater Fund, and of the benefactions of Anna T. Jeanes and of Caroline Phelps Stokes to aid Negro education in the United States did not materially change the educational deprivation which largely affected most blacks.[15]

IV THE FEDERAL INTERVENTION:
AN OVERVIEW OF EARLY EFFORTS

Federal land grants for schools in America go back as far as 1785, and land and cash grants were made during much of the 19th century. The problems of the American South generated

[11] See generally, Samuel C. Parker, The History of Modern Elementary Education (Boston: Ginn, 1912).

[12] "Yet much of the controversy and rancor which surround Lancaster are to be attributed to the very controversial nature which the education of the poor assumed in the 19th century; to the advent of popular instruction; to the unmanageable urban demos; and to the multiplicity of problems which were posed in plans for and the opposition to instruction of the children of the poor, and to the articulation of a philosophy to justify the undertaking." F. Cordasco, "Introduction," Joseph Lancaster, Improvements in Education (New York: Augustus M. Kelley, 1973 [orig. 1803]).

[13] See The Crusade for Children, 1853–1928: A Review of Child Life in New York During 75 Years (New York: The Children's Aid Society [1928]).

[14] Many of the works are reprinted in F. Cordasco, ed., The Social History of Poverty: The Urban Experience. See also, Allen F. Davis, Spearheads for Reform: The Social Settlements and the Progressive Movement, 1890–1914 (New York: Oxford University Press, 1967).

[15] See Bullock op. cit., passim.

much of the Federal concern, particularly in the matter of racially segregated schools. The Freeman's Bureau (1865) established by the Congress poured over $5 million into southern education between 1865 and 1871, but did not replace local and private effort; and the founding (1867) of Howard University (Washington, D.C.) as a black university, by the federal government is another example of early federal intervention.[16] Federal aid to American education can be best understood by highlighting major legislation from its beginnings down to 1964, e.g.:

1785   Commencement of aid to territories for education by endowment of schools with public lands.

1787   Commencement of endowment of public institutions of higher education with public lands—Northwest Ordinance: "Schools and the means of education shall forever be encouraged."

1862   The First Morrill Act—initiated federal policy of aid to states for agricultural and industrial education through land grants for colleges.

1874   Introduction of the principle of federal-state matching of funds for education.

1887   Hatch Act—encouraged scientific investigation in agriculture.

1890   The Second Morrill Act—introduction of federal grants of money for college instruction in specified areas of learning.

1914   Smith-Lever Act—matching of funds for agricultural and home economics instruction.

1917   The Smith-Hughes Act—began policy of promoting vocational education below college level through assistance with teachers' salaries.

1918   Rehabilitation training for disabled veterans.

1919   Federal surplus property available to educational institutions.

1920   The National Defense Act of 1920—direct relationship between the federal government and educational institutions.

1920   Smith-Bankhead Act—federal-state cooperation in vocational rehabilitation; education for people disabled in industry.

1935   National Youth Administration—employment for college students.

1941   Lanham Act—provided educational assistance for schools in communities affected by the federal government's activities.

[16] See Carter G. Woodson, op. cit.

1943   Vocational Rehabilitation Act—aid for disabled veterans.

1944   The Servicemen's Readjustment Act—G.I. Bill, educational aid for veterans.

1946   George-Barden Act—extended Smith-Hughes Act by increasing appropriation.

1946   National School Lunch—gave funds and food to public and non-public schools; school milk program added in 1954.

1950   The National Science Foundation Act—promoted progress in science through scholarships and fellowships in fields of science.

1950   Federal Impact Laws (P.L. 815 and P.L. 874)—extended the Lanham Act of 1941; provided assistance to communities affected by activities of the federal government for construction and operation of schools.

1952   National Science Foundation—fellowship program.

1958   The National Defense Education Act—provided for graduate fellowships in education—science, mathematics, foreign languages, counseling and guidance, educational technology.

1961   Peace Corps Act—supplied teachers and technicians to underdeveloped nations.

1962   Manpower Development and Training Act—up-to-date training for the unemployable.

1963   Health Professions Educational Assistance Act—construction of facilities and student loans.

1963   Higher Education Facilities Act of 1963—grants to all colleges, public and private, for improvement of facilities.

1963   Vocational Education Act of 1963—construction of vocational schools with expanded offerings; extended Impact Laws (1950) and NDEA (1958).[17]

The significance of 1964 lies in the fact that the Economic Opportunity Act of 1964 initiated the war on poverty under a federal auspice with the schools as the major agency of reform. In this sense, it represented a decisively new role for the Federal government in that it squarely confronted the problems of poverty and the inequality of educational opportunity.[18]

[17] For a fuller schema, see Sidney W. Tiedt, *The Role of the Federal Government in Education* (New York; Oxford University Press, 1966), pp. 195–198.

[18] For the background of the Economic Opportunity Act and its tendentious formulation and enactment, see Daniel P. Moynihan, *Maximum Feasible Misunderstanding: Community Action in the War on Poverty* (New York: Free Press, 1969). See also, John F. Hughes, *Equal Educational Opportunity: A New National Strategy* (Bloomington: Indiana University Press, 1972).

V THE JOHNSONIAN WAR ON POVERTY: FEDERAL PROGRAMS FOR THE POOR IN THE 1960s

The presidencies of John F. Kennedy (1960–1963) and Lyndon B. Johnson (1963–1968) witnessed the initiations and implementation of broad programs of domestic social reformation; the programs affecting education (although undergoing continual change) have largely been continued during the presidency of Richard M. Nixon (1969–   ).

The major catalyst of this new awareness and direct federal intervention was the Civil Rights agitation and ideological struggle out of which emerged the enactment of the Civil Rights Act of 1964. The principal educational legislation enacted by the Congress in the 1960s included:

1964	Economic Opportunity Act
1964	Civil Rights Act
1965	Elementary and Secondary Education Act
1965	Higher Education Act
1966	Adult Education Act (Amendments, ESEA)
1967	Bilingual Education (Title VII of ESEA)
1967	Education Professions Development Act
1968	Vocational Education Act Amendments
1968	Juvenile Delinquency and Control Act[19]

Each of the acts includes many components, and many of the acts were (and are) being amended to meet new needs. The *Economic Opportunity Act* included Headstart, different facets of community action programs, the Job Corps, Vista; the *Elementary and Secondary Education Act*, in a broad range of titles, addressed itself to meeting the educational needs of socio-economically deprived children (In 1969, ESEA expended $1.314 billion); the *Education Professions Development Act* brought together under a single administrative management all programs concerned with educational personnel. Capsule descriptions of selected programs follow:

[19] See generally, *Catalog of Federal Domestic Assistance: Compiled by the Office of Economic Opportunity.* (Washington: OEO, 1969); and *Listing of Operating Federal Assistance Programs Compiled During the Roth Study* (Washington: Government Printing Office, 1969).

ADULT BASIC EDUCATION

Authorizing Legislation:

Adult Education Act of 1966, Title III of the Elementary and Secondary Education Amendments 1966 (20 U.S.C. 1206, PL 89–750, 80 Stat. 1218).

Fiscal Year Funding:

$45,000,000 total (1969), of which $7,000,000 is for special projects and $2,000,000 is for teacher training.

Program Description:

Grants are provided to support state efforts to help adults learn such fundamentals as reading, writing, and arithmetic and thus qualify for occupational training and better employment. Supported programs provide instruction below the eighth grade level to persons 16 years old and over who are not enrolled in school.

BILINGUAL EDUCATION

Authorizing Legislation:

Bilingual Education Act (20 U.S.C. 880b, P.L. 90–247).

Fiscal Year Funding:

$7,500,000 (1969).

Program Description:

Programs are designed to meet the educational needs of children aged three to eighteen who have limited English-speaking ability and who come from environments where the dominant language is not English. Proposals may be submitted by an institution of higher education applying jointly with one or more local education agencies. Proposals may be submitted simultaneously to the state education agency and to Washington.

COMMUNITY SERVICES AND CONTINUING EDUCATION

Authorizing Legislation:

Higher Education Act of 1965, Title I (PL 89–329, 20 U.S.C. 1001).

Fiscal Year Funding:

$9,500,000 (1969).

Program Description:

This program provides grants to states to enable them to apply the resources of public and private institutions of higher education to the solution of community programs and by encouraging institutions to undertake programs of research and training in community problems. The goal is to make the university an integral part of the community.

EDUCATION RESEARCH AND DEMONSTRATION

Authorizing Legislation:

The Economic Opportunity Act of 1964 as amended.

Fiscal Year Funding:

$5,500,000 relate in some way to education (1969).

Program Description:

Research supported in education by the Office of Economic Opportunity is for the purpose of developing new approaches to meet better the special needs of the poor. Community action research and demonstration programs in education emphasize the direct involvement of the poor in their own education. New curricula, methods, and materials, supplemental educational programs, and functional alternatives to traditional classroom procedures are developed to create programs with greater relevance to the needs of the poor. Through these projects, OEO tests alternative methods and provides models of education programs for the poor in all age groups. Research in the preschool area is sponsored separately by Project Headstart.

EDUCATIONAL TALENT SEARCH

Authorizing Legislation:

Higher Education Act of 1965, Title IV–A (PL 89–329) as amended, as rewritten by the Higher Education Amendments of 1968 (PL 90–575, 20 U.S.C. 1068).

Fiscal Year Funding:

$4,000,000 (1969).

Program Description:

Through this program, young people who have been bypassed by traditional educational procedures are offered options for continuing their education. Contracts are awarded to projects that (1) identify disadvantaged youths who possess exceptional potential for post-secondary educational training and encourage them to complete high school and undertake further education, (2) publicize existing forms of financial aid; and (3) encourage high school or college dropouts who possess demonstrated aptitude to re-enter school. Contracts of up to $100,000 are awarded annually.

EQUAL EDUCATION OPPORTUNITIES—SCHOOL DESEG-REGATION—TECHNICAL ASSISTANCE AND TRAINING

Authorizing Legislation:

Civil Rights Act of 1964 (42 U.S.C. 2000).

Fiscal Year Funding:

$10,797,000 for total civil rights programs; approximately $9,000,000 for training of school personnel (1969).

Program Description:

Institutions of higher education may apply for technical assistance and financial support for programs to set up short-term or regular-session institutes to train school personnel to deal effectively with school desegregation problems and for operating consulting centers on such problems.

HEADSTART

Authorizing Legislation:

Economic Opportunity Act of 1964 as amended.

Fiscal Year Funding:

$323,000,000 total budget (1969):

$206,000,000 for year-round program and $90,000,000 for summer program; $6,000,000 for research and $15,-000,000 for training.

Program Description:

Headstart is a multi-faceted preschool program for three to five year-olds providing educational activities, health, psychological and social services. Parent involvement is stressed. Employment opportunities as teachers' aides and other positions are offered to parents and other neighborhood residents. The core of the program is the child development center, made up of an outdoor play area as well as one or more classrooms serving 15 children each. Each classroom is staffed by a teacher and two aides, one of whom is a volunteer. The regular program provides a range of services for eight months per year on a part- or full-time basis. A summer program for the benefit of children who are to enter kindergarten or first grade in the Fall operates during school vacation. Headstart also sponsors training for staff members, designed to increase their skills and ability to fulfill their responsibilities. Colleges and universities often conduct or coordinate these programs.

HEADSTART FOLLOW THROUGH

Authorizing Legislation:

Economic Opportunity Act of 1964 as amended (42 U.S.C. 2781).

Fiscal Year Funding:

$30,000,000 (1969).

Program Description:

Follow Through is designed to continue the gains made by deprived children who have participated in Headstart or other preschool training. Children in Kindergarten and the early elementary grades continue participation in a program of comprehensive instructional, health, nutrition, psychological social work, and parent involvement services. Universities and colleges may participate in the development of programs for the youngsters. In 1969, 14 universities ran model programs.

LOCAL INITIATIVE EDUCATION

Authorizing Legislation:

The Economic Opportunity Act of 1964, as amended.

Fiscal Year Funding:

An estimated $13,400,000 was spent in 1969 by local action programs for school-age and adult basic education.

Program Description:

A program for both children and adults to develop innovative and successful methods of providing compensatory education, to extend the efforts of the public schools, and to encourage adaptation of effective techniques by the Office of Education and other organizations concerned with teaching disadvantaged individuals. Locally developed programs supported include school-age and adult basic education programs. School-age projects provide supplementary education for poor in-school youth. A wide variety of support activities, linking in-school functions, are included. Projects fall into two general groupings: those aimed at improving academic achievements and motivation, and those with broader goals (*e.g.* stimulating parental interest in their children's education, change in the schools, or comprehensive community action through the vehicle of compensatory education. Community-based adult education projects normally offer remedial instruction designed to assist students to reach the eighth and/or twelfth grade performance level, and may also teach English as a second language. Although basic literacy and computational skills are frequently taught by means of functional subject matter, curricula and methods are diverse.

TEACHER CORPS

Authorizing Legislation:

Higher Education Act of 1965, Title V–B; Extended Education Professions Development Act, Part BI, as amended.

Fiscal Year Funding:

$15,000,000 (1968).

Program Description:

The Teacher Corps was created to strengthen the educational opportunities available to children in areas having concentrations of low-income families and to encourage colleges and universities to broaden their programs in teacher preparation.

UPWARD BOUND

Authorizing Legislation:

Economic Opportunity Act of 1964, Title II, as amended (PL 88–452).

Fiscal Year Funding:

$24,117,301 for 1969–70 school year.

Program Description:

Upward Bound is a program to motivate and prepare potentially capable, low income high school students to seek a college education. Students take a concentrated summer course (lasting generally from six to eight weeks) during which they usually live on the campus of the sponsoring institution. During the regular school year, students return to their homes, but may receive special tutoring or counselling from persons connected with their Upward Bound project or may participate in a variety of cultural and other activities designed to reinforce the gains of the summer. Students continue their participation from the time they enter the program (usually when they are high school sophomores or juniors) up to the Fall after their high school graduation. Project personnel assist them in applying to a college and in obtaining sufficient financial aid to remain in school. Consideration is also given to projects at the eighth and ninth grade levels. Individual projects vary widely since curricula are developed by grantee institutions. For both summer and winter phases, however, curricula are designed to foster those intellectual qualities, skills, and attitudes necessary for success in college. Cultural, recreational, and physical activities are provided in addition to formal classes. Grants are made to academic institutions to conduct programs.

Title I is the major component of the Elementary and Secondary Education Act of 1965. It supplies funds to public education agencies to help them meet the needs of educationally deprived pupils. Through 1968, the program's third year of operation, the Congress had appropriated more than $3 billion for distribution through Title I.

Never in the course of recorded history has a nation expanded as much money in the attempt to eradicate poverty; and, in the recognition of the educational disadvantage suffered by the children of the poor, no nation has attempted so ambitious a program of compensatory and remedial education.

VI THE PROMISE OF THE 1970s

Daniel P. Moynihan has called the 1960s "the heartbreaking decade;" certainly, the enormity of the decade's program created problems and failures. The 1970s have been characterized as a decade of consolidation:

In assigning a label to the seventh decade of the twentieth century, historians will have a wide range of descriptive terms from which to choose. Within the field of education, however, the choice could hardly be a difficult one, for it has most assuredly been the decade of the disadvantaged child, especially the young disadvantaged child. Although programs were not formulated and fielded to any extent before the middle of the decade, the theorizing, the research, and the assimilation of available information that were the necessary precursors of programmatic efforts were engaged in with great fervor from approximately 1960 until and beyond the time that programs became operational. . . . At the beginning of the seventies, education for the disadvantaged child might be described as being in a period of *consolidation*. The easy days are over, and with their departure went some of the confusion and frenzy that characterized our endeavors for several years. What is left is more than enough to work with and grow with—namely, a sound theoretical base for interest in the effects of early experience, an awareness of the need to search for new concepts in terms of which to structure operating programs, and a recognition of the need to search for ways to organize the learning environment so as to sustain as well as stimulate growth. Actually, most of the serious workers in the field are relieved at having the onus of unrealistic expectations removed. Things are now in better perspective.[20]

Any attempt to evaluate the programs means the confrontation of an enormous and proliferating literature;[21] but some major landmarks in evaluation are available.[22]

[20] Bettye M. Caldwell in Jerome Hellmuth, ed., *Disadvantaged Child: Compensatory Education, A National Debate* (New York: Brunner/Mazel, 1970), pp. v, vii.

[21] See F. Cordasco, "Poor Children and Schools," *loc. cit.*, and Meyer Weinberg, *The Education of the Minority Child* (Chicago: Integrated Education Associates, 1970). An overview of the literature is in D. Alloway and F. Cordasco, *Minorities in the American City: A Sociological Primer for Educators* (New York: David McKay, 1970).

[22] See generally, Edward L. McDill, *et al. Strategies for Success in Compensatory Education: An Appraisal of Evaluation Research* (Balti-

VII EPILOGUE

The United States of American celebrates its bicentennial in 1976. Almost from the genesis of its national history, Americans have struggled with the problems of implementing the ideals of the nation's founders.

It is in the schools that the society has laboriously sought the enfranchisement of its citizenry; and the programs which have been articulated out of the society's War On Poverty have addressed themselves (however inadequately) to the eradication of racism, to the stimulus of ethnic pride, and to the authenticity of equal educational opportunity for all its children. The awareness born of the Civil Rights Movement, the dismantling of *de jure* segregated school systems, and the interventionist programs in behalf of the poor in the 1960s, all, attest to a maturity in American society which augurs well for the future.

The promise of compensatory education was substantially to redress prevailing inequality between the education of the affluent and the poor, but its failure thus far to do so is evident from the experience of the past decade. Why? Because our nation could not or would not fulfill this commitment?

The effective education of disadvantaged children is a goal genuinely cherished by a large porportion of the American people, but it is patent that many of our citizens are indifferent or opposed to its realization. Indeed, there are those who explicitly advocate a European-type of limited "class education" for the children of the poor. . . . Could it be, despite professions to the contrary, that this negation of the goal of educational equality reflects values that really are commanding in our country?

---

more: The Johns Hopkins Press, 1969). For Title I (ESEA), see *Education of the Disadvantaged: An Evaluative Report on Title I, Elementary and Secondary Education Act of 1965.* Fiscal Year 1968 (Washington: Government Printing Office, 1970). For Headstart, see Victor G. Cicirelli, *et al., The Impact of Headstart on Children's Cognitive and Affective Development* (Westinghouse Learning Corporation and Ohio University, 1969). A literature has grown up around the controversial, James Coleman, *et al., Equality of Educational Opportunity* (Washington: Government Printing Office, 1966), for which see a special issue of the *Harvard Educational Review,* vol. 38 (Winter 1968). The "Summary" of the "Coleman Report" is reprinted in F. Cordasco, *et. al., The School in the Social Order* (Scranton: International Textbook, 1970).

The institution of education is an interacting and highly dependent unit of the whole society, decisively influenced by the values that there prevail. Considering the unparalleled resources that our nation can and does marshal in pursuit of what are clearly priority goals—as in space, in Vietnam, in the production of munitions—our persistent failure to develop good school programs for most children of the poor necessarily raises questions about the position of this goal in our national scale of values.

Compensatory education, after a decade of development, is beset by many important issues of educational theory and practice. Most fundamental to its further development, however, is whether the effective education of disadvantaged children is— or can be made—an imperative value of American society.[23]

[23] Doxey A. Wilkerson in Jerome Hellmuth, ed., *op. cit.*, p. 34.

Puerto Ricans on the Mainland: The Educational Experience

*The Legacy of the Past and
the Agony of the Present*

PUERTO RICANS ON THE MAINLAND: THE EDUCATIONAL EXPERIENCE

THE MIGRATION AND MAINLAND EXPERIENCE: AN OVERVIEW

In February 1971, the U.S. Census Bureau published its November 1969, sample-survey estimate that the fifty states and the District of Columbia had 1,454,000 Puerto Rican residents —811,000 born on the island, 636,000 born in the states and district, 1,000 in Cuba, and 6,000 elsewhere. In March 1972, the Census Bureau released preliminary and a few final state population totals from the 1970 census for three categories—persons of Spanish language, persons of Spanish family name, and Puerto Ricans. Puerto Rican counts were for three states only— New York (872,471; 5% of the state population); New Jersey (135,676; 2% of the state population; and Pennsylvania (44,535).

Puerto Ricans have been on the mainland for many years; in the 19th century, a small colony of Puerto Ricans, gathered largely in New York City, worked for the independence of the island. After the annexation of the island in 1898 by the United States, a continuing migration to the mainland began. In 1910 some 1,500 Puerto Ricans were living in the United States; by 1930, they numbered close to 53,000. The migration was reversed during the depression of the 1930s; and again was substantially impeded by World War II in the early 1940s. After the end of World War II (and concurrent with the advent of cheap air transport) it increased steadily until it reached its peak in the early 1950s (in 1953, *304,910* persons left the island and *203,307* returned, leaving a net balance of *74,603*). The state of the economy on the mainland has always been an indicator of the migration. The decline in Puerto Rican migration to

the mainland in 1970 and continuing into 1971 was precisely
due to economic hardship in the states.[1]

In a prescient book on Puerto Rican Americans, the Jesuit
sociologist, Rev. Joseph P. Fitzpatrick, observes that Puerto
Ricans have found it difficult to achieve "community solidarity"
and suggests that they may work out adjustment "in very new
ways" differing from those of past immigrants (technically, as
American citizens, Puerto Ricans are migrants to the mainland
United States); and Father Fitzpatrick cogently observes:

> A book about the Puerto Ricans in mainland United States,
> with a special focus on those in New York City, is very risky
> but also is very necessary. It is risky because the Puerto Rican
> community is in a state of turbulent change in a city and a
> nation which are also in a state of turbulent change. So many
> different currents of change affect Puerto Ricans at the present
> time that it is foolhardy to attempt to describe this group ade-
> quately or put them into focus. Nor is it possible to point out
> clearly any one direction in which the Puerto Rican community
> is moving in its adjustment to life on the mainland. Its directions
> are often in conflict, and no single leader or movement has given
> sharp definition to one direction as dominant over others. . . .
> What is most needed at this moment of the Puerto Rican exper-
> ience, both for Puerto Ricans and other mainland Americans, is
> perspective: a sense of the meaning of the migration for every-
> one involved in that migration, for the new-comers as well as the
> residents of the cities and neighborhoods to which the Puerto
> Ricans come.[2]

[1] For Puerto Rico passenger traffic for fiscal years 1940–1969, see the
reports of the Puerto Rico Planning Board. The major source of informa-
tion on Puerto Rican migration is the Department of Labor, Migration
Division, Commonwealth of Puerto Rico. See further, H. C. Barton, Jr.,
"The Employment Situation in Puerto Rico and Migratory Movements
between Puerto Rico and the United States," Summary of Proceedings:
Workshop on Employment Problems of Puerto Ricans (Graduate School
of Social Work, New York University, 1968). See also, The New York
Puerto Rican: Patterns of Work Experience. U.S. Department of Labor.
Bureau of Labor Statistics [Middle Atlantic Regional Office], New York,
1971.

[2] Joseph P. Fitzpatrick, Puerto Rican Americans: The Meaning of
Migration to the Mainland (Englewood Cliffs, N.J.: Prentice Hall, 1971),
p. xi. The Puerto Rican migration is, in many ways, a unique phenomenon
for the United States. "The Puerto Ricans have come for the most part
in the first great airborne migration of people from abroad; they are
decidedly newcomers of the aviation age. A Puerto Rican can travel from
San Juan to New York in less time than a New Yorker could travel from
Coney Island to Times Square a century ago. They are the first group to

How varied the Puerto Rican experience on the mainland has been can be best indicated by the sharp contrasts provided in four juxtaposed excerpts from Puerto Rican reactions registered over a period of time.

In 1948, J. J. Osuna, the distinguished Puerto Rican educator, on a visit to New York City schools, observed:

> As far as possible something should be done in Puerto Rico to discourage migration of people who do not have occupations to go into upon their arrival in this country, or of children whose parents live in Puerto Rico and who have no home in New York. Too many people are coming, hoping that they may find work and thereby better themselves economically, and in the case of the children, educationally. It is laudable that they take the chance, but the experience of the past teaches us that as far as possible, people should not come to the continent until they have secured employment here.[3]

In 1961, Joseph Monserrat, at the time Director of the Migration Division, Commonwealth of Puerto Rico, in speaking on "Community Planning for Puerto Rican Integration in the United States," cautioned that:

> If all Puerto Ricans were to suddenly disappear from New York City, neither the housing problem nor other basic issues confronting the city would be solved. In fact, without the Puerto Ricans, New York would be faced with one of two alternatives: either "import" people to do the work done by Puerto Ricans (and whoever was imported from wherever they might come would have to live in the very same buildings Puerto Ricans now live in for the simple reason that there is nothing else); or industries would have to move to other areas where there are workers, causing a severe economic upheaval in the city. Obviously, neither one is a viable solution. Nor will the stagnation of the past resolve our dilemma. . . . The Puerto Rican, although he comes from a close knit neighborhood in the Commonwealth,

---

come in large numbers from a different cultural background but who are, nevertheless, citizens of the United States. They are the first group of newcomers who bring a cultural practice of widespread intermingling and intermarriage of people of many different colors. They are the first group of predominantly Catholic migrants not accompanied by a native clergy. Numerous characteristics of the Puerto Ricans make their migration unique." (Fitzpatrick, p. 2)

[3] J. J. Osuna, *Report on Visits to New York City Schools* [Government of Puerto Rico]. Reprinted in F. Cordasco and E. Bucchioni, *Puerto Rican Children in Mainland Schools: A Sourcebook for Teachers* (Metuchen, N.J.: Scarecrow Press, 1968), pp. 227–239.

has found the best possibility for social action and self-improve-
ment on the city-wide level. The community of Puerto Ricans is
not the East Side or the South Side. It is New York City, Lorain,
Chicago, Los Angeles, Middletown. City living is learned living.
The migrants must be helped to learn the facts of city life and
how to function effectively as a pressure group in a pressure
group society.[4]

Both of these statements are in stark contrast to the ideology
of revolution and separatism evident in the animadversions
which follow. First, from a spokesman for "La Generación
Encojonada:"

Violence is the essence of a colonial society. It is established
as a system in the interests of the ruling classes. Colonial society
"is the meeting of two forces, opposed to each other by their
very nature, which in fact owe their originality to that sort of
substantification which results from and is nourished by the
situation in the colonies. Their first encounter was marked by
violence and their existence together . . . was carried on by dint
of a great array of bayonets and cannon." Puerto Rican history
has been witness to this violent confrontation between people and
oppressor. We see it in daily events: in schools, churches, fac-
tories, the countryside, in strikes, demonstrations, and insurrec-
tions. As soon as an individual confronts the system, he feels its
violence in the way of life colonialism imposes on him: the
feudal-type exploitation in the countryside, the capitalist exploitation in the cities.

The lifeblood of every colonial society is the profit it offers to
its exploiters. Its basis is the authority of an exploiting system—
not the authority that comes from a majority consensus, but the
paternal authority with which a minority tries to justify a system
beneficial to it. Around that system is built a morality, an ethic,
rooted in the economic co-existence of colonizers and colonized.
Thus the system envelops itself in forms that create the illusion
of sharing, of a brotherhood and equality that don't exist. The
Puerto Rican elections held every four years exemplify this. We
must not confuse the ox with the fighting bull, the causes with
the problem, the root with the branches.[5]

[4] Joseph Monserrat, "Community Planning for Puerto Rican Integration
in the United States," [An Address at the National Conference on Social
Welfare, Minneapolis, Minnesota, May 1961]. Published in F. Cordasco
and E. Bucchioni, *op. cit.*, pp. 221–226.

[5] Juan A. Silén, *We, The Puerto Rican People: A Story of Oppression
and Resistance* (New York: Monthly Review Press, 1971), pp. 118–119.
Originally, *Hacia una Visión Positiva del Puertorriqueño* (Rio Piedras:
Editorial Edil, 1970).

And from a theorectician for the Young Lords Party, spawned in the socio-pathology of the urban *barrio*:

> To support its economic exploitation of Puerto Rico, the United States instituted a new educational system whose purpose was to Americanize us. Specifically, that means that the school's principal job is to exalt the cultural values of the United States. As soon as we begin using books that are printed in English, that are printed in the United States, that means that the American way of life is being pushed . . . with all its bad points, with its commercialism, its dehumanization of human beings.
>
> At the same time that the cultural values of America are exalted, the cultural values of Puerto Rico are downgraded. People begin to feel ashamed of speaking Spanish. Language becomes a reward and punishment system. If you speak English and adapt to the cultural values of America, you're rewarded; if you speak Spanish and stick to the old traditional ways, you're punished. In the school system here, if you don't quickly begin to speak English and shed your Puerto Rican values, you're put back a grade—so you may be in the sixth grade in Puerto Rico but when you come here, you go back to the fourth or fifth. You're treated as if you're retarded, as if you're backward—and your own cultural values therefore are shown to be of less value than the cultural values of this country and the language of this country.[6]

It is no accident that this strident voice registers anger particularly with the schools; for, it is in the schools that Puerto Rican identity is subjected to the greatest pressures, and it is the educational experience on the mainland which, for Puerto Ricans, is generally bad and from which despair and alienation emerge. It is in mainland schools that the dynamics of conflict and acculturation for Puerto Ricans are best seen in clear perspective; and it is a grim irony that, generally, educational programs for Puerto Ricans have failed despite the multitudinous

[6] David Perez, "The Chains that have been Taken-off Slaves' Bodies are put Back on their Minds." *Palante: Young Lords Party* [Photographs by Michael Abramson; Text by Young Lords Party and Michael Abramson] (New York: McGraw Hill, 1971), pp. 65–66. Palante is the Spanish equivalent of "Right On" or "Forward." The Young Lords Party is a revolutionary political organization formed in New York City in 1969. The concerns of the Young Lords Party range from prisons and health care to sexism; they have cleaned up the streets of *El Barrio*, organized free breakfast programs for school children, and conducted door-to-door testing for lead poisoning and tuberculosis. See Frank Browning, "From Rumble to Revolution: The Young Lords," *Ramparts* (October 1970); and Richard C. Schroeder, *Spanish-Americans: The New Militants*. Washington: Editorial Research Reports, 1971.

educational experiments encapsulated in those new attentions born in Johnsonian America to the culture of the poor and the massive programmatic onslaughts on poverty. In the Puerto Rican mainland communities, there has been a subtle shift (following Black models) from civil rights and integration to an emphasis on Puerto Rican power and community solidarity.

And the Puerto Rican poor in their urban barrios have encountered as their chief adversaries the Black poor in the grim struggle for anti-poverty monies and for the participative indentities on Community Action Programs (funded by the Office of Economic Opportunity) which are often the vehicles and leverages of political power in the decaying American cities; additionally, a Puerto Rican professional presence in schools and a myriad of other institutional settings has been thwarted by exiled middle-class Cuban professionals. "Most of the Cubans are an exiled professional middle-class that came to the United States for political reasons. They are lauded and rewarded by the United States government for their rejection of Communism and Fidel Castro. The Cubans lean toward the political right, are fearful of the involvement of masses of poor people. Being middle-class they are familiar with 'the system' and operated successfully in this structure. They are competitive and upwardly mobile. They have little sympathy for the uneducated poor." (Hilda Hidalgo, *The Puerto Ricans of Newark, New Jersey.* Newark: *Aspira*, 1971, p. 14)

It is hardly strange that the Puerto Rican community has looked to the schools, traditionally the road out of poverty, as affording its best hope for successfully negotiating the challenges of an hostile mainland American milieu.

THE EDUCATIONAL EXPERIENCE OF PUERTO RICANS: THE BITTER LEGACY OF THE PAST

The Children of the Past

American schools have always had as students children from a wide variety of cultural backgrounds; and the non-English speaking child has been no stranger in American urban classrooms. If we are to understand the problems which Puerto Rican children encounter in mainland schools, it is instructive to look at the experience of other children (non-English speaking and culturally different) in American schools. A huge literature (largely ignored until recently) exists on the children of immigrants in the schools. No document on this earlier experience is more impressive than the *Report of the Immigration Commission* (1911) whose *Report on the Children of Immigrants in Schools* (vols., 29–33) is a vast repository of data on the educational history of the children of the poor and the schools.[7] By 1911, 57.5% of the children in the public schools of 37 of the largest American cities were of foreign-born parentage; in the parochial schools of 24 of these 37 cities, the children of foreign-born parents constituted 63.5% of the total registration.[8] "To the immigrant child the public elementary school was the first step away from his past, a means by which he could learn to assume the characteristics necessary for the long climb upward."[9] And by 1911, almost 50% of the students in secondary schools were of foreign-born parentage.[10] In American cities, the major educational challenge and responsibility was the immigrant child.

In the effort to respond to the needs of the immigrant child, it is important to note that no overall programs were developed to aid any particular immigrant group. Although there was little agreement as to what Americanization was, the schools were committed to Americanize (and to Anglicize) their charges.

Ellwood P. Cubberley's *Changing Conceptions of Education* (1909), which Lawrence A. Cremin characterizes as "a typical progressive tract of the era,"[11] saw the immigrants as "illiterate, docile, lacking in self-reliance and initiative, and not possessing the Anglo-teutonic conceptions of law, order, and government . . .," and the school's role was (in Cubberley's view) "to assimilate and amalgate."

What efforts were made to respond to the needs of immigrant children were improvised, most often directly in answer to

[7] United States Immigration Commission. *Report of the Immigration Commission*, 41 vols. (Washington: Government Printing Office, 1911). *The Report on the Children of Immigrants in Schools* (vols. 29–33) has been reprinted with an introductory essay by F. Cordasco (Metuchen, N.J.: Scarecrow Reprint Corp., 5 vols, 1970):

[8] The U.S. Immigration Commission, *op. cit. Abstracts. The Children of Immigrants in Schools*, vol. II, pp. 1–15.

[9] Alan M. Thomas, "American Education and the Immigrant," *Teachers College Record*, vol. 55 (April 1954), pp. 253–267.

[10] See footnote 8, *supra*.

[11] Lawrence A. Cremin, *The Transformation of the School* (New York: Knopf, 1961). "To Americanize, in this view, was to divest the immigrant of his ethnic character and to inculcate the dominant Anglo-Saxon morality." (*Ibid.*)

specific problems; almost never was any attempt made to give the school and its program a community orientation. The children literally left at the door of the school their language, their cultural identities, and their immigrant subcommunity origins.[12] A child's parents had virtually no role in the schools;[13] and the New York City experience was not atypical in its leaving the immigrant child to the discretion of the individual superintendent, a principal, or a teacher.

Against such a lack of understanding and coordinated effort in behalf of the children of the poor it is hardly strange that the general malaise of the schools was no where more symptomatic than in the pervasive phenomenon of the overage pupil who was classed under the rubric "retardation" with all of its negative connotations. The Immigration Commission of 1911 found that the percentage of retardation for the New York City elementary school pupils was 36.4 with the maximum retardation (48.8%) in the fifth grade.[14] The Commission observed:

> . . . thus in the third grade the pupils range in age from 5 to 18 years. In similar manner pupils of the age of 14 years are found in every grade from the first of the elementary schools to the last of the high schools. It will, however, be noted that in spite of this divergence the great body of the pupils of a given grade are of certain definite ages, the older and younger pupils

[12] See the autobiography of Leonard Covello, *The Heart is the Teacher* (New York: McGraw-Hill, 1958). It is significant to note that Covello, as an immigrant boy in East Harlem, was more influenced by the work of the evangelist, Anna C. Ruddy, who had devoted years to social work in the East Harlem Italian community, than by the public schools. See Anna C. Ruddy (pseudonym, Christian McLeod), *The Heart of the Stranger* (New York: Fleming H. Revel, 1908); see also Selma Berrol, "Immigrants at School: New York City, 1900–1910," *Urban Education*, vol. 4 (October 1969), pp. 220–230.

[13] See Leonard Covello, *The Social Background of the Italo-American Child: A Study of the Southern Italian Mores and their Effects on the School Situation in Italy and America*, edited and with an introduction by F. Cordasco (Leiden, The Netherlands: E. J. Brill, 1967); and also, Leonard Covello, "A High School and its Immigrant Community: A Challenge and an Opportunity," *Journal of Educational Sociology*, vol. 9 (February 1936), pp. 331–346. "Where the Italian community was studied, it was subjected to the ministrations of social workers (who concentrated on the sociopathology inevitable in a matrix of deprivation and cultural conflict) or to the probing of psychologists who sought to discern and understand the dynamics of adjustment." F. Cordasco, *Italians in the United States* (New York: Oriole Editions, 1972), p. xiii.

[14] United States Immigration Commission. *The Children of Immigrants in Schools, op. cit.*, vol. 32, p. 609.

being in each case much less numerically represented. It may, therefore, be assumed that there is an appropriate age for each grade. This assumption is the cardinal point in current educational discussion in regard to retardation. If it were assumed that there is a normal age for each grade, then the pupils can be divided into two classes—those who are of normal age or less and those who are above the normal age. The latter or overage pupils, are designated as "retarded."[15]

At best, it is a dismal picture whose poignant and evocative pathos is etched in the faces of the children imprisoned in the cheerless classrooms of the era.[16] It could have been otherwise: in the lower East Side of New York City the efforts of District School Superintendent, Julia Richman, at the turn of the century, pointed in the more rewarding directions of community awareness, of building on the cultural strengths which the child brought to the school; and the near quarter-century tenure (1934–1957) of Leonard Covello at Benjamin Franklin High School in New York City's East Harlem, dramatically underscored the successes of the community centered school. But Julia Richman and Leonard Covello were the exceptions, not the rule; and it is hardly fortuitous that they came out of the emerging Jewish and Italian subcommunities, for these very identities help explain their responsiveness to the immigrant child.[17]

[15] *Ibid.*, pp. 608–609.

[16] See many of the contemporary photographs taken by the social reformer Jacob Riis and reproduced in his books, particularly, *The Children of the Poor* (New York: Scribner, 1892); and generally, in F. Cordasco, ed., *Jacob Riis Revisited: Poverty and the Slum in Another Era* (New York: Doubleday, 1968). See also, Robert Hunter, *Poverty* [particularly the chapter entitled, "The Child"] (New York: Macmillan, 1904); and John Spargo, *The Bitter Cry of the Children* (New York: Macmillan, 1907).

[17] Julia Richman has, unfortunately, been neglected; she is one of the great urban school reformers in a period marked by hostility and contempt for the children of the poor. All of her writings are important. See particularly the following: "A Successful Experiment in Promoting Pupils," *Educational Review*, vol. 18 (June 1899), pp. 23–29; "The Incorrigible Child," *Educational Review*, vol. 31 (May 1906), pp. 484–506; "The Social Needs of the Public Schools," *Forum*, vol. 43 (February 1910), pp. 161–169; "What Can Be Done For The Backward Child," *The Survey*, vol. 13 (November 1904), pp. 129–131. For Covello, see footnote 13, *supra*; and his "A Community Centered School and the Problem of Housing," *Educational Forum*, vol. 7 (January 1943); and "A Principal Speaks to His Community," *American Unity*, vol. 2 (May 1944).

PUERTO RICAN CHILDREN IN THE SCHOOLS

The Early Years

It is in the perspectives of these earlier experiences that the educational failures of the Puerto Rican child are to be viewed and understood. Committed to policies of Americanization, the schools neglected the cultural heritage of the Puerto Rican child, rejected his ancestral language, and generally ignored his parents and community. And these policies were in keeping with the traditional practices of the schools.

The Puerto Rican community in New York City is the largest on the mainland, and its experience would be essentially typical of other mainland urban communities. As early as 1938, the difficulties of the Puerto Rican child in the New York City schools are graphically (if passingly) noted:

> Many Puerto Rican children who enter the public schools in New York speak or understand little English. The children who are transferred from schools in Puerto Rico to those in New York are usually put back in their classes so that they are with children who are two or three years younger than they are. Americans who are teaching Puerto Rican children express the opinion that these children have had less training in discipline and in group cooperation than American children. Lacking the timidity of many of the children in this country, they sometimes act in an unrestrained and impulsive manner. One large agency in the settlement, which has dealt with Puerto Rican children for many years, reported that under proper conditions Puerto Rican children are responsive, easily managed, and affectionate. In contrast to this, another large institution said that for some reason which they could not explain the Puerto Rican children were more destructive than any group of children with whom they had had contact. All the evidence obtainable shows the relation of unsatisfactory home conditions to difficulties at school. During the past few years the desperate economic condition of these families has caused them to move so frequently that it has often been difficult to locate the children when they did not attend school.[18]

[18] Lawrence R. Chenault, *The Puerto Rican Migrant in New York City.* With a Foreword by F. Cordasco (New York: Russell & Russel, 1970; originally, Columbia University Press, 1938), p. 146. See also, C. P. Armstrong, *Reactions of Puerto Rican Children in New York City to Psychological Tests. A Report of the Special Committee on Immigration*

In December, 1946, Dr. Paul Kennedy, then President of the New York City Association of Assistant Superintendents, appointed a committee "to study and report on the educational adjustments made necessary by the addition of the 400,000 Puerto Ricans who have lately become residents of this city." The surprizingly comprehensive report prepared by this committee considered native backgrounds; migration to the mainland; problems of assimilation; the education of the Puerto Rican pupil; and made a number of recommendations.[19] That the report was achored in the past is evident in its caution that "Although the Puerto Rican is an American citizen, the adjustment he must make in this city is like that of immigrants to this country from a foreign land." The report counted "13,914 pupils enrolled [June 1947; by October 1970, 260,040 were enrolled] in the public elementary and junior high schools of the city who originally came from Puerto Rico;" and further grimly observed: "there is no doubt but that many pupils coming from Puerto Rico suffer from the double handicap of unfamiliarity with the English language and lack of previous educational experience, sometimes approaching complete illiteracy. Malnutrition and other health deficiencies contribute to the educational problem of the schools. The overcrowding at home and the restlessness on the street carry over into the school in the form of nervousness, extreme shyness, near tantrums, and other behavior characteristics which are the more difficult for the teacher to understand because of the language barrier." (p. 38)

---

and Naturalization. (State of New York: Chamber of Commerce, 1935) which Chenault used but (in keeping with the temperment of the time) noted "It is not the purpose of this study to raise the question of the innate ability of the migrant." Perhaps, the earliest notice of Puerto Ricans in New York City is the unpublished typescript (14 pp.) on file in the office of the National Urban League, William E. Hill, *Porto Rican Colonies in New York* (1929).

[19] *A Program of Education for Puerto Ricans in New York City. A Report Prepared by a Committee of the Association of Assistant Superintendents* (New York: Board of Education, 1947). The report (106 pp.) was mimeographed with what appears to be a very limited circulation. "For years, boys and girls from Puerto Rico have entered the public schools of New York City. For the most part they came into Spanish Harlem, arriving in such small numbers that their admission to school was accepted routinely. Together with other non-English speaking children from European countries, they were placed in "C" classes, and gradually assimilated into the regular program of the school. There was no reference then to a 'Puerto Rican problem' in the schools." (p. 3)

The Committee, also undertook the first study of "reading progess" among Puerto Rican pupils who were new admissions to the elementary and junior high schools; and it made a series of recommendations, chief among which was the establishment of special classes ("C" classes) for Puerto Rican children "for whom at least a year's time is needed for preliminary instruction and language work before they are ready for complete assimilation in the regular program." Although the report was generally neglected, it represented the first systematic study undertaken on the mainland to call attention to the needs of Puerto Rican children.

Attention has been called to J. J. Osuna's *Report on Visits to New York City Schools* in 1948 (see footnote #3). In 1951, a Mayor's Committee on Puerto Rican Affairs in New York City was convened and considered the needs of Puerto Rican pupils;[20] and in 1953, Dr. Leonard Covello, then Principal of Benjamin Franklin High School in East Harlem, consolidated and articulated into schematic form for consideration the various proposals which had been made up to that time to deal with the needs of Puerto Rican children in the schools.[21]

Finally, in 1953, the New York City Board of Education presented in booklet form the results of a study initiated by its Division of Curriculum Development. This brief report indicated a new awareness of the importance of using Spanish in instructing Puerto Rican children, of the need for knowledge of Puerto Rican cultural backgrounds, and of the need for bilingual teachers.[22] But it equally made clear the critical need for a fully developed educational program for Puerto Rican children; and it served as a prologue to the *Puerto Rican Study* which was initiated in 1953.

[20] "Puerto Rican Pupils in American Schools." *Mayor's Committee on Puerto Rican Affairs in New York City. Report of the Subcommittee on Education, Recreation and Parks* (New York: 1951). Part of the report is reprinted in Cordasco and Bucchioni, *op. cit.*, pp. 246–253.

[21] Leonard Covello, "Recommendations Concerning Puerto Rican Pupils in our Public Schools" (Benjamin Franklin High School, May 1, 1953). This is an invaluable document, and is published in Cordasco and Bucchioni, *op. cit.*, pp. 254–259. Attention should also be called to *Education of the Non-English Speaking and Bilingual (Spanish) Pupils in the Junior High Schools of Districts 10 and 11, Manhattan* (June 1952), prepared at the request of New York City Assistant Superintendent Clare C. Baldwin. The report noted that "every school in Districts 10 and 11 has some Puerto Rican children on its register."

[22] *Teaching Children of Puerto Rican Background in New York City Schools* (New York: Board of Education, 1953).

The Puerto Rican Study

The Puerto Rican Study was, for its time, one of the most generously funded educational studies every undertaken.[23] The Fund for the Advancement of Education provided a grant-in-aid of a half million dollars and "contributions equivalent in amounts authorized by the Board of Education made the study a vital operation in the school system." (*Foreword*) It was not completed until 1957, and it was finally published in April 1959. It is, unquestionably, the fullest study ever made of the Puerto Rican educational experience on the mainland; and, in a broader sense, it remains one of the most comprehensive statements yet made, not only of the Puerto Rican school experience, but of the educational experience of the non-English speaking minority child in the American school.[24] As such it is an invaluable document in American educational historiography, with all of the contemporary relevancies which the 1960s have defined (and continuing into the 1970s) with reference to ethnicity, the minority child, the contexts of poverty, and the educational needs of the "disadvantaged" child. It is strange that, in the proliferating literature on the minority child and the schools, *The Puerto Rican Study* should have been neglected; and its neglect may be due to its appearance before the advent of the

[23] The Puerto Rican Study, 1953–1957. *A Report on the Education and Adjustment of Puerto Rican Pupils in the Public Schools of the City of New York* (New York: Board of Education, 1958). For some of the backgrounds of the report, see J. Caycee Morrison, *A Letter to Friends of Puerto Rican Children* (1955); and his "The Puerto Rican Study-What It Is; Where It Is Going," *Journal of Educational Sociology*, vol. 28 (December 1954), pp. 167–173

[24] The only comparable work is Leonard Covello's *The Social Background of the Italo-American School Child* (see footnote #13). For the contiguity and relationships of the Italian and Puerto Rican communities in East Harlem, see F. Cordasco and R. Galattioto, "Ethnic Displacement in the Interstitial Community: The East Harlem (New York City) Experience," *Phylon: The Atlanta University Review of Race & Culture*, vol. 31 (Fall 1970), pp. 302–312. *The Puerto Rican Study* was released officially by the New York City Board of Education on April 6, 1959. See *New York Times*, April 7, 1959. "Dr. John J. Theobold, The Superintendent of Schools, said that a 'substantial number' of recommendations and findings in the study had already been implemented. Teaching materials, courses of study and guides developed by the project, he said, are now being used. He said there were now 2,255 special classes for Puerto Rican children in the elementary and 346 such classes in the secondary schools." *New York Times, loc. cit.*

Johnsonian anti-poverty programs of the 1960s with their educational components, and to the inevitable fate of sponsored
reports whose implementation and evaluation are seldom realized or avoided for a variety of reasons.

The Puerto Rican Study's objectives are clearly stated:

> In a narrow sense, *The Puerto Rican Study* was a four-year
> inquiry into the education and adjustment of Puerto Rican pupils
> in the public schools of the City of New York. In a broader
> sense, it was a major effort of the school authorities to establish
> on a sound basis a city-wide program for the continuing improve-
> ment of the educational opportunities of all non-English-speaking
> pupils in the public schools.
>
> While the *Study* was focused on the public schools in New
> York City, it was planned and conducted in the belief that the
> findings might be useful to all schools, public and private, that
> are trying to serve children from a Spanish-language culture. As
> the *Study* developed, it seemed apparent that it might have
> values, direct or indirect, wherever children are being taught
> English as a second language. (p. 1)

It sought answers to the following specific problems: (1) What
are the most effective methods and materials for teaching English as a second language to newly-arrived Puerto Rican pupils?
(2) What are the most effective techniques whereby the school
can promote a more rapid and more effective adjustment of
Puerto Rican parents and children to the community and of the
community to them?

As the *Study* progressed, its staff developed two series of
related curriculum bulletins—*Resource Units* organized around
themes and designed for all pupils, and a *Language Guide
Series* which provided the content and methods for adapting the
instruction to the needs of the pupils learning English (the
Study lists the *Units* and *Series*). The *Study* also furnished a
detailed description of the Puerto Rican children; devised a
scale to rate English-speaking ability; and constructed a detailed program for the in-service education of teachers (Chapter
17).[25]

[25] *The Resource Units* and the *Language Guide Series* are invaluable
aids for the teacher who is looking for materials for the instructional
program for Puerto Rican children; equally valuable (and developed as
part of *The Puerto Rican Study*) is Samuel M. Goodman, *Tests and Testing: Developing a Program for Testing Puerto Rican Pupils in Mainland
Schools* (New York: Board of Education, 1958). Admittedly, *The Resource Units* and the *Language Guide Series* were intended (in their

The Recommendations of The Puerto Rican Study

Its recommendations ("Where *The Puerto Rican Study* Leads") are both a blueprint and design for effectively meeting the needs of Puerto Rican children, and they impinge on all those facets of the experience of the minority child which are interrelated and which, if neglected, impede social growth and cognitive achievement. Simply listed (without the capsuled rationales which accompany them), they represent a skeletal construct as meaningful today as when they were formulated:

1. Accept *The Puerto Rican Study*, not as something finished, but as the first stage of a larger, city-wide, ever improving program for the education and assimilation of non-English-speaking children.
2. Take a new look at the philosophy governing the education of the non-English-speaking children in New York City schools.
3. Recognize that whatever is done for the non-English-speaking child is, in the long run, done for all the children.
4. Use the annual school census as a basic technic in planning the continuing adaptation of the schools to the needs of the non-English-speaking pupils.
5. Recognize the heterogeneity of the non-English-speaking pupils.
6. Formulate a uniform policy for the reception, screening, placement, and periodic assessment of non-English-speaking pupils.
7. Keep policies governing the grouping of non-English-speak-

---

emphases) to facilitate a more rapid adjustment to the American way of life (in keeping with the ethos of *The Puerto Rican Study* and its period), but this does not detract from their value as cognitive aids. *The Puerto Rican Study* and its ancillary materials are a complete conspectus for the education of Puerto Rican children measured against the principles discussed in Theodore Andersson and Mildred Boyer, *Bilingual Schooling in the United States.* 2 vols. (Austin, Texas: Southwest Educational Development Laboratory, 1970); and Vera P. John and Vivian M. Horner, *Early Childhood Bilingual Education* (New York: Modern Language Association of America, 1971). Notice should also be made of the materials describing the programs at the Bilingual School (Public School #211, Bronx, N.Y.) which incorporate many of the recommendations of *The Puerto Rican Study.* The most completely developed Bilingual School in the United States is Public School #25 (Bronx, N.Y.) whose programs are essentially based on the recommendations of *The Puerto Rican Study.*

ing pupils flexible. Place the emphasis upon serving the needs of the individual pupil.

8. Place special emphasis on reducing the backlog of retarded language learners.

9. Recognize "English as a second language" or "the teaching of non-English-speaking children" as an area of specialization that cuts across many subject areas.

10. Use the curricular materials developed by *The Puerto Rican Study* to achieve unity of purpose and practice in teaching non-English-speaking pupils.

11. Capitalize on the creative talent of teachers in finding ways and means of supplementing and of improving the program for teaching non-English-speaking pupils.

12. Recognize and define the school's responsibility to assist, counsel, and cooperate with the parents of non-English-speaking pupils in all matters pertaining to the child's welfare.

13. Take a new look at the school's opportunity to accelerate the adjustment of Puerto Rican children and their parents through advice and counsel to parents on problems normally considered to be outside the conventional functions of the school.

14. Staff the schools to do the job: to help the new arrival to make good adjustment to school and community; to help the non-English-speaking child to learn English and to find his way successfully into the main stream of the school's program.

15. Staff the proper agencies of the Board of Education to maintain a continuing program for the development and improvement of curricular materials and other aids to the teaching of non-English-speaking pupils.

16. Staff, also, the proper agencies of the Board of Education, and set in motion the processes to maintain a continuing assessment or evaluation of technics, practices and proposals.

17. Take a new hard look at the psychological services provided for non-English-speaking children, especially for Puerto Rican children.

18. Through every means available, make it clear that the education of the non-English-speaking children and their integration in an ever changing school population is the responsibility of every member of the school staff.

19. Maintain, improve, and possibly expand the program of in-service preparation initiated through *The Puerto Rican Study* for training special staff to assist in accelerating the program for non-English-speaking children.

20. In cooperation with the colleges and universities of Metro-
    politan New York, create a dynamic program to achieve
    unity of purpose and more adequate coordination of effort
    in the education of teachers and of other workers for
    accelerating the program in the schools.
21. Use the varied opportunities available to develop an ever
    improving cooperation between the Department of Educa-
    tion in Puerto Rico and the Board of Education in New York
    City.
22. In cooperation with the responsibile representatives of the
    government of the State of New York, continue to explore
    the mutual interests and responsibility of the city and the
    state for the education and adjustment of non-English-
    speaking children and youth.
23. Think of the City of New York and the Commonwealth of
    Puerto Rico as partners in a great enterprise.

No full scale implementation of *The Puerto Rican Study* was
attempted. Much of what the *Study* recommended appears
again in the New York City Board of Education *Educating Students for whom English is a Second Language: Programs, Activities, and Services* (1965), a pamphlet-review of subsequent
programs which emphasized teacher training programs, particularly the exchange of teachers between New York and Puerto
Rico. All kinds of reasons can be advanced for the failure to
implement *The Puerto Rican Study*, and these might include
teacher and Board of Education resistance; the struggles which
were to ensue over community participation, and decentralization; the rapidly politicizing community/school contexts with
their attendant ideological quarrels; the absence of qualified
personnel; and the accelerating growth of the Puerto Rican
community which simply overwhelmed many of the schools.
Whatever the reasons (and no one reason or a combination
of reasons provides an acceptable explanation), the *Study*
was more than a million dollar white elephant. Its achievements (however incompletely implemented) included the
following:

1. Developed two series of related curriculum bulletins—*Resource Units* and *Language Guides*—for use in teaching
   English to non-English-speaking pupils. These are keyed to
   New York City courses of study but may be easily adapted
   to courses of study in other school systems. They are
   adapted to the maturity level of children, grade by grade
   in the elementary school, and in terms of need for special

instruction in English during the early secondary school years.

2. Developed a guide for teaching science—resource units and sample lessons—to Puerto Rican pupils who are still trying to learn English; and a guide for teaching occupations to teen-age Puerto Rican pupils in high school who wish to qualify for occupational employment.

3. Developed a battery of tests, measures, and data-gathering technics for use with Puerto Rican pupils in the mainland schools. Among these were a tape-recorded test for measuring the ability of non-English-speaking pupils to understand spoken English, a scale for rating ability to speak English, a bilingual test of arithmetic, and a process for screening new arrivals and for following their progress through periodic reviews.

4. Though an educational-ethnic-social survey of several thousand children in New York City elementary and junior high schools, obtained a profile of the characteristics of pupils of Puerto Rican background in relation to other pupils in the same grades and schools.

5. Through testing thousands of pupils, obtained estimates of the potential abilities as well as of the present performance of Puerto Rican pupils in relation to their peers i.e., other pupils of the same age and grade in the same schools.

6. Through a variety of studies of individual children from kindergarten through the tenth grade or second year of high school, gained revealing information concerning the problems of Puerto Rican children in achieving cultural-educational-social adjustment in New York City schools.

7. Through a survey of the relations of schools to Puerto Rican parents, defined the problems confronting the schools, formulated criteria for determining the schools' role, and made some estimate of the cost in terms of personnel needed to help facilitate or accelerate the cultural adjustment of Puerto Rican parents.

8. Through analysis of previously established positions and of new positions established on an experiemental basis, developed criteria for determining the necessity for special staff in schools to enable them to serve the needs of Puerto Rican and foreign-born or non-English-speaking children.

9. Through two years of experimentation with different procedures, developed proposals for an in-service program to reach all teachers required to teach non-English-speaking pupils.

10. Through participation in three summer workshops sponsored in part by the Board of Education of the City of New

York at the University of Puerto Rico, formulated proposals
for the development of the annual workshop as a continuing means of promoting better mutual understanding and
cooperation between the school system of New York city
and the school system of Puerto Rico.

11. Through the surveys and testing of thousands of children,
devised a plan for obtaining a uniform census of all Puerto
Rican and foreign-born children in the schools. Administration of census, through consecutive years, will give the
Board of Education data for predicting with a high degree
of accuracy pending changes in the ethnic composition of
pupil population by school, school district, school level,
borough and city.

12. The gradation of ability to speak English as defined by the
Puerto Rican Study in its scale for rating ability to speak
English was used by the Commissioner of Education of the
State of New York in defining non-English-speaking pupils
as a basis for the distribution of additional state aid ap-
propriated by law. (pp. 9–10)

In themselves, these achievements (and the recommendations) were to become the measuring criteria against which
continuing needs were to be delineated.[26]

[26] The failure to implement *The Puerto Rican Study* led to great
agitation and continuing demands from the Puerto Rican community. The
first Citywide Conference of the Puerto Rican Community (April 1967)
in its published proceedings (*Puerto Ricans Confront Problems of the
Complex Urban Society*, New York City: Office of the Mayor, 1968)
presented recommendations for the education of Puerto Rican children,
essentially a repetition of those made by *The Puerto Rican Study*. And
in 1968, Aspira (an organization founded in 1961 by the Puerto Rican
Forum to promote higher education for Puerto Ricans) convened a
national conference of Puerto Ricans, Mexican-Americans, and educators
on "The Special Educational Needs of Urban Puerto Youth." The conference's published report (*Hemos Trabajado Bien*. New York: Aspira,
1968), in its recommendations, reiterated most of those of *The Puerto
Rican Study*. The Aspira conference also commissioned a report on
Puerto Ricans and the public schools, Richard J. Margolis, *The Losers: A
Report on Puerto Ricans and the Public Schools* (New York: Aspira,
1968). This brief report chronicles visits to sixteen schools in seven cities
and "makes no explicit recommendations. Its purpose is to put the
problem in sharper focus and on wider display, not to promote any single
set of solutions." Margolis' report is a devastating indictment of those
schools which neglected Puerto Rican children, and of programs which
largely were encrusted with all the bitter abuses of the past: it appears
inconceivable that the practices he describes could have been occurring a
decade after the publication of *The Puerto Rican Study*.

BEYOND THE PUERTO RICAN STUDY

The Bilingual Education Act

Much of the effort in behalf of the educational needs of Puerto Rican children in the 1960s must be viewed and understood in the light of the massive federal interventions in education largely initiated by the enactment of the Elementary & Secondary Education Act of 1965, and its subsequent amendements.

The passage by the Congress in 1968 of the Bilingual Education Act (itself, Title VII of the ESEA) reaffirmed and strengthened many of the recommendations of *The Puerto Rican Study*, even though the *Study* had largely fallen into undeserved neglect. The struggle for a national bilingual education act represented a continuing fight against the ethnocentric rejection of the use of native languages in the instruction of non-English-speaking children;[27] and, in our view, the successful enactment of the Bilingual Education Act represented a movement away from the "ethnocentric illusion" in the United States that for a child born in this country English is not a foreign language, and virtually all instruction in schools must be through the medium of English; even more importantly, the Act was a national manifesto for cultural pluralism and bicultural education, and in this sense may prove the most socially significant educational legislation yet enacted.

The Act recognized "the special education needs of the large numbers of children of limited English speaking ability in the United States," and declared "it to be the policy of the United States to provide financial assistance to local educational agencies to develop and carry out new and imaginative elementary and secondary school programs designed to meet these

[27] See F. Cordasco, "The Challenge of the non-English-Speaking Child in American Schools," *School & Society*, vol. 96 (March 30, 1968), pp. 198–201, which is an adaptation of testimony before the Committee on Education and Labor of the U.S. House of Representatives in support of the proposed Title VII (June 29, 1967); and for the history of the legislation, see F. Cordasco, "Educational Enlightenment Out of Texas: Toward Bilingualism," *Teachers College Record*, vol. 71 (May 1970), pp. 608–612; and F. Cordasco, "The Bilingual Education Act," *Phi Delta Kappan*, vol. 51 (October 1969), p. 75. The Bilingual Education Act, Title VII (P.L. 90–247; 20 U.S.C. 880b) authorized the expenditure of $25 million in Fiscal 1971.

special educational needs." The main priorities of the Act are the provision of equal educational opportunities for non-English-speaking children; the strengthening of educational programs for bilingual children; and the promotion of bilingualism among all students. A great number of programs have come into being as a result of the Act, and although the programs are of differing (and in some instances of dubious) quality, the programs affirm the practicability of meeting the needs of the non-English-speaking child.[28] Use of the principles and recommendations of *The Puerto Rican Study* would strengthen programs for Puerto Rican children, as even a casual examination would affirm.

The Realities of Program Implementation

In the last analysis, it is the program which addresses itself to the educational needs of the Puerto Rican child which must be evaluated with recommendations made for its continuing improvement. The evaluation of a particular program for Puerto Rican children in a large urban school district and the recommendations which were made for its improvement and expansion are, in themselves, instructive: they delineate the contemporary educational experience for the Puerto Rican child, and they point the way to meet the needs.

The recommendations which are subjoined derive from a study and evaluation of the educational programs for Puerto Rican students underway in the Jersey City (N.J.) school district in 1971–1972.[29] Over 5,000 Puerto Rican pupils (out of a total school register of some 38,000) were in the city's schools. The recommendations provide a profile of contemporary Puerto Rican educational experience (practice that lends itself to improvement), generally encountered on the mainland.

[28] For a list and description of some of the programs, see "Bilingualism," *The Center Forum*, vol. 4 (September 1969), p. 20–26; and Vera P. John and Vivian M. Horner, *op. cit.*, pp. 15–107.

[29] F. Cordasco and Eugene Bucchioni, *Education Programs for Puerto Rican Students:Evaluation and Recommendations* (Jersey City: Board of Education, 1971), pp. 27–37.

PROGRAM RECOMMENDATIONS

Elementary Level

1. The basic recommendation to be made for the elementary schools involves the establishment of functional bilingual programs wherever there are Puerto Rican students in attendance. The basic premise of bilingual education involves the use of Spanish to provide instruction in most curriculum areas when English is not the mother tongue of the children and when there is insufficient fluency in English to profit from school instruction in that language. Thus, for example, instruction in basic curriculum areas such as mathematics, social studies, *etc.* would be in Spanish. At the same time that instruction is given in the basic content areas in Spanish, an intensive program in the teaching of English as a second language must be conducted. As children develop greater fluency in English, additional instruction in the basic curriculum areas should be given in English. This approach would assist children in becoming equally fluent in both Spanish and English, and at the same time it would also assist children to develop the appropriate knowledges and skills in curriculum areas other than Spanish and English. Bilingual education should also provide for the teaching of Spanish as a second language for those children who are dominant in English. Such programs should begin in September 1972.

At the present time in the bilingual classes in the Jersey City schools, this approach is not in widespread use. Teachers who speak Spanish are used for the most part to interpret what the English speaking teacher has said, and (as noted above) often at the same time, a practice resulting in considerable confusion. In addition, the practice of assigning two teachers to a room, one of whom functions as an interpreter, represents poor utilization of personnel, both educationally and financially.

2. The bilingual program recommended by the evaluators would also necessitate the regrouping of participating children more carefully. In addition to using the traditional criteria for grouping, in a bilingual education program it is necessary to develop parallel classes or sections of children who are dominant in either English or Spanish. In developing bilingual programs, however, it is essential that priority be given in class assignment to children who are dominant in Spanish, rather than to those dominant in English, because the greatest immediate need exists for children who are dominant in Spanish and who cannot derive as much educational value as possible from school programs conducted solely in English.

3. It is recommended that two schools [perhaps, Public School No. 2 and Public School No. 16 in view of the very large number of Puerto Rican students in attendance] develop complete bilingual programs beginning with the kindergarten and including each grade in the school. In other schools, bilingual classes should be established as needed.

4. A committee on bilingual education at the elementary school level should be established immediately in order to plan for the development of bilingual programs in Public Schools Nos. 2 and 16, and in other schools of Jersey City where there are large Puerto Rican enrollments. The bilingual education committee will also give attention to the development of a bilingual curriculum encompassing the usual curriculum areas as well as the teaching of English as a second language, the teaching of Spanish as a second language, and the history and culture of Puerto Rico as an integral part of the elementary school curriculum. The present Hispanic Culture Committee is a beginning; but it must deal with a Puerto Rican studies curriculum and only ancillarily with Hispanic cultures in general. Membership on the committee should include parents, teachers, principals and should also make provision for student input.

5. A city wide Puerto Rican advisory council composed of parents, high school and college students and community leaders should be established. The advisory council can advise school officials on the needs, aspirations, sentiments and responses of the Puerto Rican community insofar as educational matters are concerned. The existence of a community advisory council will assist in making public schools with large numbers of Puerto Rican students "community schools," furnishing educational and other much needed services to the Puerto Rican community. Such an advisory council on a city wide basis [and articulated with local advisory councils for specific schools] will provide much needed community participation in education in Jersey City for the Puerto Rican community.

6. Parochial schools with large numbers of Puerto Rican students should also participate in special programs funded with federal monies.

7. All communications from school officials to parents should be available in both English and Spanish.

8. Additional Puerto Rican personnel should be recruited for positions at all levels in the public schools including teachers, principals, school secretaries, a curriculum specialist, teacher aides, *etc*. Special attention should be turned immediately to the employment of a curriculum specialist in bilingual education.

9. At the present time, no city wide coordinating effort involving existing bilingual programs is available in Jersey City. It is

recommended, therefore, that a city wide office at the level of coordinator for bilingual education be established. This office will have jurisdiction over planning, developing, implementing, supervising and evaluating all bilingual education programs, programs in the teaching of English as a second language, and other special service programs for Puerto Rican elementary school children and high school students. The office would also provide liaison with the Puerto Rican community.

10. Bilingual classes as envisaged in recommendation #1 should also be made available in the Summer of 1972. [The period January 1972 to June 1972 should be used as a planning period for the bilingual programs to be established in the Summer and Fall of 1972].

11. It is recommended that provision be made for the establishment of a continuing consultancy in the implementation of the recommendations contained in this report. Consultants would work with school officials and members of the Puerto Rican community in the implementation of the recommendations and would assist in the development of other programs and special services that may be needed by the children of the Puerto Rican community.

12. Parent education programs conducted in both Spanish and English should be developed for the Puerto Rican community.

13. An in-service program for teachers and other school personnel should be developed as soon as possible. Current and past efforts in Jersey City in the areas of in-service courses include the offering of a course in "Teaching English as a Second Language" that was to be given in the 1970/71 school year, beginning in November, 1970 and a request to develop and finance an "In-Service Course Involving Philosophy, Approaches and Methodology of Bilingual Education," to be given during the 1971/72 school year. In-service efforts should be expanded, and should include both professionals participating directly in bilingual programs or English as a second language programs as well as other professionals in the Jersey City Public Schools who may not be participating in special programs for Puerto Rican children but who do work with Puerto Rican children in regular classes. Such an extensive in-service program might be developed and offered during the regular school year, or might be given as a special summer institute for participating personnel.

14. Greater numbers of Puerto Rican student teachers should be recruited from Jersey City State College. An expanded student-teaching practicum drawn from the cadres of Puerto Rican students at Jersey City State College represents an important source for recruiting larger numbers of Puerto Rican personnel for employment in the Jersey City Public Schools.

15. A continuing and expanded liaison between the Jersey City Public Schools and Jersey City State College is recommended. Here, an important beginning and model [Title VII, at School No. 16] has been provided by Professor Bloom and Jersey City State College personnel.

Secondary Level

1. The city wide Community Advisory Council described in recommendations for elementary schools should also turn its attention to secondary education and make recommendations relevant to the educational needs of Puerto Rican high school students in Jersey City.

2. A testing and indentification program should be developed at the secondary level. Such a program would attempt to identify Puerto Rican students in need of intensive instruction in English as a second language or in other important school subjects such as reading.

3. A special committee to deal with secondary education for Puerto Rican students should be established, with the membership drawn from teachers, principals, guidance personnel and other school professionals; and including parents and students from the Puerto Rican community. The committee should give special attention to the current basic offerings: industrial arts, college preparatory, business and general studies. It should consider ways of increasing the holding power of the secondary schools so that greater numbers of Puerto Rican students remain in high school and graduate.

4. Special work study programs for Puerto Rican students might be developed in connection with the basic offerings now available. Such work study programs could become a very significant phase of the industrial arts and business education programs, and should, consequently, carry high school credit.

5. An immediate attempt should be made to increase the number of Puerto Rican students in the college preparatory program. This can be done by teachers, guidance personnel and administrators. More information about current high school programs should be made available, and students should become familiar with the implications of selecting specific programs and the out-of-school consequences of enrollment in any given program. In addition, talent-search programs might be initiated to increase the number of Puerto Rican students entering college.

6. Secondary school teachers should paticipate in in-service programs dealing with the education of Puerto Rican students.

7. It is recommended that high school students having little fluency in English be given basic instruction in Spanish in the

various classes required in the four curricula. Instruction in Spanish would be in addition to intensive instruction in reading, writing and speaking English as a second language. When high school students have achieved a sufficient degree of fluency in English, they may then receive all or most of their instruction in English. Bilingual education at the high school level at the present time is essential, and it is especially important when large numbers of students are dominant in Spanish rather than in English. It should be remembered that it was not possible to secure from school officials data concerning the number of Puerto Rican high school students dominant primarily in Spanish.

8. At present, a secondary school curriculum committee is working on a course of study in Puerto Rican history. The work of this committee should be accelerated and a course of study in Puerto Rican history and culture should be developed as rapidly as possible. The committee might then turn its attention to the development of a course of study dealing with the Puerto Rican experience on the mainland. At present, there are no student members of this committee. Students should be a significant and contributing part of this committee. Indeed, greater participation by high school students in the decisions affecting their school careers is vital, and it becomes especially crucial when there are large numbers of students dropping out of high school programs as is true for many Puerto Rican students.

9. The high schools should make available to all high school students without cost all special examinations such as the National Education Development Tests or the College Boards. Such examinations now require the payment of fees by candidates taking them. There may be many Puerto Rican and other students unable to take the examinations which require the payment of fees because of inability to afford the funds required.

10. The continuing consultancy referred to in recommendations for elementary schools should encompass secondary education as well as elementary education.

11. It is recommended that an experimental program involving independent study be instituted for those students who are considering leaving high school before graduation. This program would provide the opportunity for independent study under supervision, for which credit leading to a high school diploma would be given. Such a program would also provide for attendance in organized classes in the high schools, especially where remedial or advanced programs are required. Students would participate in developing their programs. Such supervised independent study programs could be related to jobs which students leaving high school before graduation may have secured.

12. It is recommended that additional Puerto Rican personnel

be recruited for employment in Jersey City secondary schools. The two Puerto Rican guidance counselors at Ferris High School are an important beginning.

These recommendations are, essentially, reaffirmations of the cogency of those made years earlier in *The Puerto Rican Study*. One cannot help but wonder how differently meaningful educational opportunity for Puerto Rican children may have been had *The Puerto Rican Study* been implemented. In its cautions and admonitions, *The Puerto Rican Study* was prophetic: "A study, however good, never solves problems. At best if finds solutions that will work. To translate proposed measures into practice is the greater task. At the very best it will take three to five years to translate the proposals of *The Puerto Rican Study* into an effective program. . . . The real question is, how rapidly can the school system move? . . . there are thousands of Puerto Rican children in New York City schools who have been here two, three, four or more years and are still rated as language learners. The task is twofold—to salvage as many as possible of those currently retarded, and to reduce the numbers that thus far have been added annually to the list. The time to begin is now—A year gone from a child's life is gone forever." (p. 237)

BIBLIOGRAPHY OF SELECTED REFERENCES

I *General Bibliographies*

Cordasco, Francesco with Eugene Bucchioni and Diego Castellanos. *Puerto Ricans on the United States Mainland: A Bibliography of Reports, Texts, Critical Studies and Related Materials* (Totowa, New Jersey: Rowman & Littlefield, 1972). An annotated bibliography of 754 main entries dealing with bibliographical resources; the migration to the mainland; the island experience; conflict and acculturation on the mainland; education on the mainland; and social needs encompassing health, housing, employment, and other human needs.

Cordasco, Francesco and Leonard Covello. *Studies of Puerto Rican Children in American Schools: A Preliminary Bibliography.* New York: Department of Labor, Migration Division, Commonwealth of Puerto Rico, 1967. [some 450 entries]. Also published in *Education Libraries Bulletin,* Institute of

Education, University of London, #31 (Spring 1968), pp. 7–33; and in *Journal of Human Relations*, vol. 16 (1968), pp. 264–285.

[Cordasco, Francesco]. *The People of Puerto Rico: A Bibliography.* New York: Department of Labor, Migration Division, Commonwealth of Puerto Rico [1968]. Some 500 entries.

Dossick, Jesse. *Doctoral Research on Puerto Rico and Puerto Ricans.* New York: New York University, School of Education, 1967. A classified list of 320 doctoral dissertations completed at American mainland universities.

II General Studies

Burma, John H. *Spanish-Speaking Groups in the United States.* Duke University Press, 1954. Includes a sketch of "the Puerto Ricans in New York" (pp. 156–187). Burma assumes that there is a fundamental "unity of culture" among diverse groups put together because they speak the same language. In light of the widely differing historical backgrounds which have given rise to different cultures among Spanish-speaking groups the assumption does not seem valid.

Chenault, Lawrence. *The Puerto Rican Migrant in New York City.* Columbia University Press, 1938. Reissued with a New Foreword by F. Cordasco. New York: Russell & Russell, 1970. The one book that puts together data available on the early movements to New York City of Puerto Rican migrants. Includes a discussion of the various ways these movements affect the established community and the migrants.

Cordasco, F. and David Alloway, "Spanish Speaking People in the United States: Some Research Constructs and Postulates," *International Migration Review*, vol. 4 (Spring 1970), pp. 76–79.

Cordasco, F. and Eugene Bucchioni. *The Puerto Rican Experience: A Sociological Source book.* To owa, N.J.: Rowman and Littlefield, 1973.

Fitzpatrick, Joseph P. *Puerto Rican Americans: The Meaning of Migration to the Mainland.* Englewood Cliffs, N.J.: Prentice Hall, 1971. An overview and trenchant study with materials on the dynamics of migration: the problem of identity; the family; problem of color; religion; education; welfare. See *New York Times*, September 12, 1971, p. 96.

Glazer, Nathan and **Daniel P. Moynihan.** "The Puerto Ricans." In: *Beyond the Melting Pot: The Negroes, Puerto Ricans, Jews, Italians, and Irish of New York City,* by Nathan Glazer and Daniel Moynihan. Cambridge: M.I.T. and Harvard University Press, 2nd ed., 1970. Puerto Ricans in New York City are discussed in terms of who migrates to the United States; their relationship to the island of Puerto Rico; business, professional, labor opportunities, and average earnings in New York; and the effect of migration on the culture of the migrants. The Puerto Ricans are compared and contrasted with immigrant groups. [1st ed., 1963]. The 2nd edition updates some of the material, and includes a new introductory essay and analysis.

Lewis, Oscar. *La Vida: A Puerto Rican Family in the Culture of Poverty—San Juan and New York.* New York: Random House, 1966. 669 pp. Begins with a long introduction which describes Lewis' methods, the setting, and the family involved in the study. A discussion of the theory of the "culture of poverty" is included. The rest of the book is the story of a Puerto Rican family, as told by the members of the nuclear family and some of their relatives and friends. See also Oscar Lewis; *A Study of Slum Culture: Backgrounds for La Vida.* New York: Random House, 1968. Provides the general background, data, and statistical frame of reference for *La Vida.*

Mills, C. Wright; Clarence Senior; and **Rose Goldsen.** *The Puerto Rican Journey: New York's Newest Migrant.* Harper, 1950. Reissued, New York: Russell & Russell, 1969. A carefully researched field study of the Puerto Rican population in two core areas of New York City. The study was done in 1948 by a research team of the bureau of applied social research of Columbia University. Although many of its statistics are now out of date, the book deals with basic concepts, such as the factors in "adaptation," cultural and language differences, and their influence on the progress and problems of the migrants. Includes much data on the characteristics of the Puerto Ricans in the two core areas—family, age, sex, education, occupation, income, etc.

Puerto Rican Community Development Project. Puerto Rican Forum [New York], 1964. This report was developed as the basis for an antipoverty, economic opportunity project, and is subtitled "A Proposal for a Self-Help Project to Develop the Community by Strengthening the Family, Opening Opportunities for Youth and Making Full Use of Education." The forum is a private agency, with a professional and secretarial staff of New Yorkers of Puerto Rican background. It has received some financial support from foundations to develop self-help projects as well as some public money to develop its proposal. Thus the concern in this report is to highlight the problems—income, housing, education, family, *etc.*—that confront the Puerto Rican community in New York City, though not all of its population. Data are presented to support the thesis that Puerto Ricans generally are not well off and need to make much more rapid gains in a contemporary technical, urban society such as New York. As a Forum summary indicates, the report is advanced as a rationale for a project "which takes into consideration both the problems of poverty in New York City and the complex realities of the cultural community pattern of the Puerto Rican New Yorker." The report is not intended to be a rounded picture of the total Puerto Rican population in New York City. Read from the point of view of its purpose, it is an illuminating study.

"[The] Puerto Rican Experience on the United States Mainland," *International Migration Review,* vol. II (Spring 1968). Entire issue devoted to a comprehensive account of the experience.

Sexton, Patricia. *Spanish Harlem: Anatomy of Poverty.* Harper & Row, 1965. Report by a sociologist who spent part of two years "getting acquainted" with East Harlem. Shows awareness that she is dealing with the pathologies of a minority of the area's population ("still, the majority of the people are self-supporting"). However, she does not gloss over the problems that confront many of the self-supporting, low-income urban dwellers. The book is informed by the important insight of the need for "the poor" to be involved in working out their destiny. See F. Cordasco, "Nights in the Gardens of East Harlem: Patricia Sexton's East Harlem," *Journal of Negro Education*, vol. 34 (Fall 1965), pp. 450–451; and F. Cordasco, "Spanish Harlem: The Anatomy of Poverty," *Phylon: The Atlanta University Review of Race & Culture*, vol. 26 (Summer 1965), pp. 195–196.

III   Education

Anderson, Virginia. "Teaching English to Puerto Rican Pupils," *High Points* (March 1964), pp. 51–54.

Bilingual Education: Hearings, U.S. Senate, Committee on Labor and Public Welfare. Special Sub-Committee on Bilingual Education, 90th Congress, 1st Session. Washington: U.S. Government Printing Office, Part I, May 1967; Part II, June 1967. On Title VII (Elementary and Secondary Education Act) which was enacted in 1968.

"Bilingualism," *The Center Forum*, vol. 4 (September 1969). Entire issue is given to analysis of Title VII (Elementary and Secondary Education Act), programs and related matters. Includes an important annotated bibliography.

Bucchioni, Eugene. *A Sociological Analysis of the Functioning of Elementary Education for Puerto Rican Children in the New York City Public Schools.* Unpublished doctoral dissertation, New School for Social Research, 1965.

Cordasco, Francesco. "The Puerto Rican Child in the American School." American Sociological Association *Abstract of Papers*, 61st Annual Meeting (1966), pp. 23–24.

Cordasco, Francesco. "Puerto Rican Pupils and American Education." *School & Society*, vol. 95 (February 18, 1967), pp. 116–119. Also, with some change, in *Journal of Negro Education* (Spring 1967); and *Kansas Journal of Sociology*, vol. 2 (Spring 1966), pp. 59-65.

Cordasco, Francesco. "The Challenge of the Non-English Speaking Child in the American School" *School & Society*, vol. 96 (March 30, 1968), pp. 198–201. On the proposal for the enactment of the Bilingual Education Act. (Title VII, Elementary and Secondary Education Act), with historical background.

Cordasco, Francesco. "Educational Pelagianism: The Schools and the Poor," *Teachers College Record*, vol. 69 (April 1968), pp. 705–709.

Cordasco, Francesco and Eugene Bucchioni. *The Puerto Rican Community of Newark, N.J.: An Educational Program for its Children.* Newark: Board of Education, Summer 1970. A detailed report on the implementation of a program for Puerto Rican students.

Cordasco, Francesco and E. Bucchioni. *Education Programs for Puerto Rican Students.* [Jersey City Public Schools]. Evaluation and Recommendations. Jersey City: Board of Education, 1971.

Cordasco, F. and Eugene Bucchioni. *Newark Bilingual Education Program, 1970–1971.* Newark: Board of Education, 1971. Evaluation report of a massive program for Puerto Rican students.

Cordasco, Francesco and Eugene Bucchioni. *The Puerto Rican Community and its Children on the Mainland: A Sourcebook for Teachers, Social Workers and other Professionals.* Metuchen, N.J.: Scarecrow Press, 2nd ed., 1972. "The original structuring of the text has been retained, and it is within this framework that new materials have been interpolated. New materials have been added to Part I (Aspects of Puerto Rican Culture) whose basic design is to afford a politico-cultural kaleidoscope of island life; to Part II (The Puerto Rican Family), bringing into clear focus the family's transition to mainland life; to Part III (The Puerto Rican Experience on the Mainland: Conflict and Acculturation), in bringing into sharp view the new politicization of the mainland experience; and in Part IV (The Puerto Rican Experience on the Mainland: Puerto Rican Children in North American Schools) in affording additional materials on bilingual education and in providing outlines for course content and staff-training. Appended to the bibliography are selected additional references." [Preface to the 2nd ed.]

Cordasco, Francesco and Eugene Bucchioni, "A Staff Institute for Teachers of Puerto Rican Students," *School & Society*, vol. 99 (Summer 1972).

Diaz, **Manuel** and **Roland Cintron.** *School Integration and Quality Education.* New York: Puerto Rican Forum, 1964.

Hemos Trabajado Bien. A Report on the First National Conference of Puerto Ricans, Mexican-Americans and Educators on the Special Educational Needs of Puerto Rican Youth (New York: Aspira, 1968). Includes a series of recommendations.

John, Vera P. and **Vivian M. Horner.** *Early Childhood Bilingual Education* (New York: Modern Language Association 1971). Invaluable. Includes a "Typology of Bilingual Education Models," excellent documentation and bibliography.

Margolis, Richard J. *The Losers: A Report on Puerto Ricans and the Public Schools* (New York: Aspira, 1968). An important report on visits to a number of schools with description and evaluation of programs for Puerto Rican children.

[Puerto Rican Children] "Education of Puerto Rican Children in New York City," *The Journal of Educational Sociology,* vol. 28 (December 1954), pp. 145–192. An important collection of articles.

Morrison, J. Cayce, Director. *The Puerto Rican Study: 1953–57.* New York City Board of Education, 1958. Final report of the most complete study of the impact of Puerto Rican migration on the public schools of New York City, and how schools were affecting Puerto Rican children and their parents. Though sponsored by the New York City Board of Education, matching grant-in-aid of half a million dollars from the Fund for the Advancement of Education made the study possible. Specialized studies were done within the framework of the large-scale study. These smaller studies focused on the "socio-cultural adjustment" of the children and their parents, and digests are presented in final report. About a third of the book deals with the special non-English-speaking program developed by the city school system. Description of some of the methods and materials developed is included. Study discovered some unresolved problems in the areas of learning, effective grouping of pupils, staffing those schools with Puerto Rican children, and teacher education. Study led to many research and curriculum publications, and 23 major recommendations, all designed to achieve three purposes: " * * * [developing] better understanding of the children being taught, [relating] the teaching of English to the child's cultural-social adjustment, [improving] the integration of ethnic groups through the school's program" (p. 247). With respect to the children, the major conclusion is contained in the following statement: "The children of Puerto Rican background are exceedingly heterogeneous. This is true of their native intelligence, their prior schooling, their aptitude for learning English, and their scholastic ability * * * " (p. 239). Reissued with an introductory essay by F. Cordasco (New York: Oriole Editions, 1972).

The Urban Education Task Force Report:

Summary

URBAN EDUCATION TASK FORCE REPORT: SUMMARY

These points should be borne in mind with regard to this report. First, the problems confronting urban education and its environment are *not* of sudden origin. Such problems as inadequate financing, increased enrollments, insufficient staffing, malnutrition, and discrimination have all existed for a long time. However, there are some differences—the surfacing of these problems nationally, increased awareness of their seriousness, and their interrelatedness to poverty.

Second, the picture presented of urban education and its environment is far from pleasant. However, the presentation in the documentation section is not to be construed as criticism for criticism's sake. Instead, our intent is to underscore the urgency of dealing with urban education's needs as a major national priority and to lay the foundation for our ensuing recommendations.

Third, the Task Force, deliberately chosing to reflect diversity in viewpoints, inevitably found unanimity impossible on all of the recommendations made by its committees. Hence, both majority and minority points of view are presented in this report with the intent of demonstrating alternative views on and recommendations for resolving the issues and problems identified. This report also reflects many of the suggestions for modifications made by members of the Task Force.

Worthy of mentioning is the fact that every member of the Task Force recognizes that education in this country has never been assigned an adequate priority in terms of financial, human, and material resources.

Overview of the Urban Education Problem

Urban education systems are facing a major challenge to provide appropriate learning experiences for the various life styles of vast numbers of students. The indicators of this challenge are extremely diverse in their intensity and scope: student unrest on university campuses and in the high schools, local community groups seeking control of their neighborhood schools, clashes with law enforcement agencies, complaints being filed with regard to use of Federal funds, teacher strikes, voter rejection of large city school bond issues, the proliferation of alternative plans for educating students, lack of priority for education in State and local governments. The greatest number of such indicators—intensifying each other —are taking place in our cities.

This challenge is, in turn, part of yet a broader and more complex one. Major changes have occurred in the perceptions of large numbers of American citizens, specifically the minority racial and ethnic groups, who now express their feelings of exclusion from meaningful participation in the social, economic, political, and educational institutions of our nation. The steady accumulation of evidence across a wide spectrum of human needs and rights signals that these perceptions are largely supported.

Vastly increased amounts of money are now imperative. In general, the amount of Federal money thus far added has been insufficient for the magnitude of the task confronted. Furthermore, the sustained flow of money is another problem. Complicating these problems are contradictions in terms of legislation and budget priorities at the Federal, State, and local levels which often work against urban areas and their school systems. As the cities become poorer and education becomes costlier, the probabilities increase for the inner city student to participate in only a substandard education. And it is he who should be able to secure a superior education since it constitutes his passport to economic self-sufficiency and self-realization.

However, solving the monetary problems alone is not the complete answer. Major changes must take place in the educational system as well. Compensatory education programs which are producing positive results with impoverished students usually reflect *combinations* of modified curriculum, staff development, enlightened staff attitudes, supportive services, parent support, and adequate funding. Too few of these programs are currently operating.

Education holds the promise of a one-generation-up-and-out process. That is, the poverty child does not have to repeat the poverty pattern of his parents if he receives a valid and salable education.

It is within this context that we strongly urge that the problem of urban areas should be considered as the major priority of the Administration's domestic programs. Within this priority, education—broadly conceived and with new constituencies involved—should become a first consideration. The overwhelming majority of the Task Force adopted all of the below-noted positions.

Money. Significantly increased levels of funding are needed for urban education far exceeding what current appropriations—even authorizations—now make possible. However, the criteria for securing funds must be based upon such factors as poverty indices, community determination, demonstrated capability to carry out such a program, levels of State and local efforts, the recognition of the fact that education is more expensive in the cities than elsewhere, and a clear focus on both the *inner* city areas and the suburban poverty pockets.

Concept of urban education. Education as we have typically defined it is too narrow for the impoverished constituencies with whom we are concerned. The educative process must be truly expanded in its focus to the whole individual at all educational levels. It must be conceived of as taking place any time and anywhere; focused on the whole community with genuine respect for its various needs, aspirations, and strengths; and aimed at preparing students for all the complexities of urban living.

Master plan for urban education. The only viable approach to resolving the complex problems of education in urban areas is through the development and implementation of a master plan for urban education from early childhood through higher and adult education tailored to the specific needs of a particular urban area.

Institutional changes. There must be a deliberate sequence of steps planned and implemented which will lead to institutional change within educational systems. Such a sequence should be based on a changed and expanded perspective concerinng the role(s) and function(s) of the schools and their staffing, including institutions of higher education. While the fundamental changes must be made *within* the system rather than occurring outside of it, alternative educational approaches can also contribute positively to accelerating the rate of institutional change.

Community determination. Community residents and students must have an active role in the critical decision-making concerning urban education problems. The definition of this role will need to be worked out locally within a broad and flexible set of guidelines. Regardless of the form that the community determination takes, it should contain policymaking contributions in the areas of: priorities for spending the available monies; the educational program offered; and hiring of key personnel. (Definitions which are evolved will have to be conditioned by the legal constraints of existing State and Federal legislation.)

Performance standards. Clearly stated performance standards or criteria should be established for an urban education program. These criteria should constitute a clear statement of the specific knowledges, attitudes, and skills which the students themselves are expected to demonstrate. In effect, they should describe the kinds of students the educative process intends to produce in terms of overt behaviors. Furthermore, performance criteria should be established for *all* educational staff involved in the program.

Assessment. Assessment should be an *integral* part or component of the urban education program beginning with the planning phase. Moreover, this assessment component should be designed to assure rapid and continuing feedback on the program's strengths and weaknesses and should allow for rapid modifications and adjustments to be made in the program based on student performance. Furthermore, Federal funding should be conditioned on the attainment of measurable standards of this performance by urban school agencies.

Racial and ethnic integration. Racial and ethnic integration should be a major element in all the planning and implementation phases of the urban education program and should be clearly stated as a major criterion for receiving funds. Recognizing that there is no single or simple way of achieving real integration, a community applying for funds should demonstrate how its educational plan contributes to overcoming racial and ethnic isolation. We suggest that the current thrust composed of separatism, local community control, and the demand for a recognized identity is not over the long term antithetical to the aims of integration. Rather, it constitutes an attempt to achieve through other channels what these earlier thrusts have only partially fulfilled. Still another thrust seems to be emerging which reflects neither primary reliance on public-spirited members of the white majority nor the "we'll go it alone" stance of some groups within the minorities. Instead, it reflects the effort to achieve legitimate power bases from which to negotiate as equals with the majority. This emergent thrust is potentially very promising since it concomitantly recognizes common goals and proposes a cooperative approach in achieving them. Therefore, we strongly support a broadened view of racial and ethnic integration which includes within it those actions which superficially and over the short term may seem militant.

The purposes of this report are as follows:

1. To describe and document the critical problems and needs confronting urban education.

2. To examine the extent to which the Federal government can and should extend solutions to the problems facing urban education.

3. To recommend long-term programmatic and legislative approaches needed to resolve the problems and needs identified; and also to recommend the short-term actions that can be taken under existing legislation.

PART I: THE STATE OF URBAN EDUCATION

Part I of this report considers the four major dimensions of the problem confronting urban education in Chapters 2 through 5. Specifically, they deal with the financial crisis of the urban schools; the urban environment of the students; the urban education system; and the impoverished urban student.

Two points should be borne in mind with regard to the chapters of Part I. First, rarely—if ever—has there been an attempt to show the problems of urban education in the light of their surrounding context. Instead, education and its setting are often treated as separate entities with separate problems. Since children and youth spend more time in school than they do in any other social agency, the school and its setting inevitably interact on one another. Thus, they should be interrelated when studied. Second, although it is difficult to secure data for the documentation of urban education's needs, sufficient evidence has been arrayed to delineate the major dimensions of the problem facing urban education.

Chapter 2: the Financial Crisis
of the Urban Schools

To provide the basis for the recommendation that the Federal government must assume a policy of top priority for urban areas demonstrated by massive appropriations to meet the need of educationally and economically disadvantaged families, the extent and nature of the current financial crisis is demonstrated through a documentation of the following factors:

Financial deterioration due to population migration. Generally, the high tax producers are leaving the cities while ever-increasing numbers of high tax consumers—the disadvantaged—are entering the city. The obvious result is less money available to meet greater needs.

The higher cost of urban education. It is more costly to meet the needs of the educationally deprived than those of the affluent suburban student. Compounding this problem are the higher maintenance costs and vandalism rates in the inner city.

Inequitable State aid formulas. Such formulas not only fail to recognize the disproportionate educational expenses of the cities, but compound the problem by providing central cities with less State aid per capita than is made available to the outlying areas.

Dwindling popular support and confidence in education. Adverse votes on tax measures and bond references have left many cities with drastically inadequate budgets.

Financial difficulties of non-public schools. Non-public schools have felt many of the same financial pressures as public schools. As the former are forced to close their doors, the latter have been faced with serving whole new school populations with inadequate budgets and facilities.

Minimal level and minimal effect of Federal funds. Federal aid is less than 8 percent of the average local education dollar. In addition, cities do not receive their fair share under most Federal education programs.

Without adequate funding, there is no hope for effective education in the cities. The current need for funds is as desperate as it is massive.

CHAPTER 3: THE URBAN ENVIRONMENT
OF THE STUDENTS

The urban environment of the student—as characterized by divergent values, overcrowding, underhousing, high cost of living, low levels of income, too much discrimination, too little food, and too much noise—also constitutes a major dimension of the problem confronting the schools. The environment is not static—it is dynamic. As such, the environment is potentially and continuously involved in the process of educating its residents, among them its children and youth. The educative process in the schools cannot—and should not —be separated from that in the environment. In this chapter, the major elements of this environment are identified and analyzed with respect to their influence on the student. These elements are below noted.

Health and nutrition. The urban student often suffers from malnutrition which results in inadequate health and energy levels, minimizing his efforts on demanding school tasks. He lives in a world in which the mortality rates of women and babies in birth are higher and the life expectancies of men are lower than for other Americans.

Economic status and unemployment. Unemployment, underemployment, and inadequate welfare are facts of life for many urban students. Education brings some upward mobility, but more often racial discrimination acts as an obstacle to securing education, employment, and advancement.

Housing and living conditions. The inner city student lives in poor, overcrowded housing for which a family is likely to have to over-pay.

The family. Although there are many stable families residing in such areas, the divorce, separation, and desertion rates are comparatively high in the inner cities. If not within his immediate family, then within his neighborhood, the inner city student will gain an early knowledge of problems associated with drug addiction, prostitution, and theft. He will probably develop a tough self-reliance, a spirit of cooperation, a tolerance for a high degree of noise, and a casualness in terms of daily routine. The concepts, language, and problem-solving techniques he acquires will be primarily geared to his survival in the neighborhood and the necessary interactions in and demands of his family.

CHAPTER 4: THE URBAN
EDUCATION SYSTEM

Although the argument is often offered that financial inadequacies and the conditions of the student's urban environment are the only important contributors to the urban education problem, the education system itself must bear some share of the responsibility. These problems are summarized below.

Obstacles faced by urban education systems. In addition to the great obstacle of inadequate funding, the flow of racial and ethnic minorities has created obstacles for the schools in terms of the numbers, poverty, social isolation, and lack of education of these urban immigrants. Yet while the system has generally acknowledged the problems of its numbers, it has in many cases failed to respond adequately to the needs of these individuals. The size and nature of the immigration has in turn imposed difficulties in achieving the goal of integration, increased the inadequacy of school facilities, and made the existing teacher shortage more acute. The problems of recruiting fully accredited teachers, keeping accredited experienced teachers for any length of time, and achieving a racial and ethnic balance are more sharply felt in the cities than in the suburbs.

Problems of the education system in perceiving its students. In many instances, educational systems are unable to cope with a pluralistic culture. A serious problem with many urban systems today is their lack of awareness of the effects of their own biases on their students. Possessing essentially the same general goals as previous waves of immigrants (e.g., economic security, self-respect, personal safety), the minorities today nevertheless manifest some differences in values, needs, and problems. These often unrecognized biases and unchanging expectations have often limited the system's capacity to teach effectively children who do not have the same expectations, such as being oriented to middle-class values and expectations, being "ready" for reading, and having the structural orientation that facilitates shifting from subject matter to subject matter as dictated by time blocs rather than by interest and substance. The failure of many teachers to perceive their students as they are stems from complex origins relating to the status assigned by society to teaching the disadvantaged and the levels of competency and experience of the teachers.

Problems with the system as a perception of its students, its faculty, its community. The system has major problems if significant elements of its constituency believe it is failing. Three such elements (i.e., the students, the teachers, and the general community) are identified and their perceptions discussed. The student's perception of the system's failure is reinforced through the documentation of achievement levels, drop-out rates, and instances of violence. The teacher's perception is articulated by strikes, disagreements, and a growing body of dissent literature. The community's perception of this failure is expressed by the defeat of bond issues, or general lack of support and confidence, and a growing trend toward demands for decentralization and separatism.

CHAPTER 5: THE IMPOVERISHED URBAN STUDENT

A brief analysis of the impoverished urban student is presented in terms of behaviors which often go largely unutilized in present educational programs. Proceeding from a combination of direct experience, anecdotal report, and analogical reasoning, the evidence cited is focused on three categories of behaviors of major importance to academic learning: (1) his capacity for realistic problem-solving at many levels; (2) his excellent communication capabilities which encompass the kinds of verbal abilities required by the school; and (3) his generosity, cooperation, and candor.

Appropriate programs and staff capitalize on these and other behaviors of this student with achievement as one major result. However, such programs, staff, and results occur all too infrequently.

PART II: THE FEDERAL RESPONSIBILITY

In this section, there are two points to bear in mind. One is that the Federal government is beginning to shift its focus from comparatively specific efforts in education to broad social action thrusts which encompass more than education per se. Problems in evaluating such programs have arisen as a result of their new thrusts. The other point is that the Federal role is not easily defined with regard to these broad educational programs. It is in the process of emerging and its development must take place in the midst of constitutional precedents and political realities.

Chapter 6: Problems in Evaluating the Impact of Current Federal Progams for Impoverished Populations

The major change in the Federal focus on education from the previous relatively small and specific programs affecting limited groups (e.g., NDEA) to the newer broadly conceived large social action programs (e.g., ESEA, Title I) affecting impoverished populations has not been accompanied correspondingly by a major change in the approaches being used in the evaluation of these programs.

More fundamental than the methodological problems in the evaluation of the current programs are the conceptual and political problems.

Conceptual The central conceptual problem arises from the fact that while the new programs are essentially political and social in nature, evaluators tend to approach them as though they were standard efforts at educational change.

Political. Three major problems are identified: (1) the fact that the current operating programs (e.g., ESEA, Title I) were not envisaged as vehicles for research and development in their legislative mandates; (2) the existing distribution of political power in education; and (3) the basic lack of resources—both fiscal and human.

Chapter 7: The Federal Role in Urban Education Limits and Obligations

The dimensions of the newly developing Federal role in education are described within the context of: (1) political and financial limitations; and (2) the obligation—and precedent—for the Federal government to intervene specifically where it is in the national interest to solve a particular problem. Urban education now poses such a problem.

The dimensions of the new Federal role are seen as: (1) fostering institutional change for the improvement of economic, social, health, and educational conditions of impoverished groups; (2) providing increased monies for such educational and education-related programs; and (3) becoming an advocate on behalf of impoverished groups as a result of (1) and (2).

A major question is raised concerning whether or not the Federal government has the skill and determination to redesign its education programs in ways which will solve urgent national problems of social progress and human survival. Moreover, the point is made that massive amounts of money are necessary—and only the Federal government has the resources to solve these problems.

PART III: A PLAN FOR URBAN EDUCATION

This part of the report presents the long-range recommendations on which the Urban Education Task Force places its major emphasis. In addition to the long-range recommendations, short-range recommendations are made relating to existing legislation. The latter are meant only to serve as a holding action until such time as the long-term recommendations are operative.

This report submits as its major recommendation the development in the Office of education of special landmark legislation, such as an Urban Education Act, which will be designed to fund the planning, development, and implementation of a comprehensive master plan to meet the long-range educational and education-related needs of inner city areas. To accomplish this, the Task Force recommends that the Office of Education immediately establish an Office of Programs Serving the Disadvantaged under an Associate Commissioner, to become the Bureau of Urban Education with broader mandates upon the passage of an Urban Education Act.

Part III of this report discusses the long-term recommendations relevant to the Urban Education Act in Chapters 8 through 11—governing the educational program, the authority structure, funding principles, and the cost respectively. The short-term recommendations are presented in Chapter 12.

Minority viewpoints are presented for those recommendations on which more than one alternative was offered. However, the recommendations stated first represent the large majority of the Task Force members.

CHAPTER 8: AN URBAN EDUCATION
ACT—THE EDUCATIONAL PROGRAM

Authorized by an Urban Education Act, urban areas should plan and develop comprehensive master plan proposals for the redesign of educational programs and supportive services which would set forth specific educational and social goals, the educational services, and performance standards for the improvement of education at all levels within the area to be served, with special emphasis for inner city students.

Scope of the master plan. In order to provide the inner city student with an equal opportunity to function successfully in the mainstream, his education must not be merely equal, but be superior to that in the suburbs. The master plan must accordingly reflect the most enriched definition of education and relate that education to current urban problem areas including integration, housing, employment, recreation, and health.

To ensure this superior education, general criteria should be established—preferably in the legislation itself but it could be done administratively—which would be concerned with: a broadened definition of education; the use of existing and heretofore largely unutilized instructional resources; the use of financial resources at all levels of public and private sources; a clearly articulated needs statement indicating a knowledge of the target area and its problems on a need priority basis; a general set of objectives for a total program which will consider those problems of the city which have direct bearing on the process of education; a specific set of educational objectives to be met by the educational program of the master plan; a full description of the program; plans for continuous assessment of the program in terms of student performance; and plans for an evaluation of the over-all institutional performance.

Levels of the education program. The master plan should encompass all educational levels from early childhood through adult. While all levels should be fully and equally treated in the plan, certain long-range considerations might be afforded the early childhood level, while short-term considerations might affect secondary and higher education.

Educational program components. The educational program of the master plan should include at a minimum the following program and program-related components:

1. PLANNING. This component should be continuous with various phases, such as initial design, preliminary implementation, feedback, modification, etc.

The planning framework should assume *integration* as a vital aspect of education and should take all feasible steps toward this goal. The planning framework must also assume *institutional change* as a necessity, not for the sake of change, but as the implementation of new aspects which have been proven more effective than those in use. Plans should consider gains, not only for students, but for the *total community* through a wide use of resources. *Pre-grant performance* should be indicated and planners should be required to use existing funds to demonstrate performance prior to receiving developmental and operational funds.

2. PERSONNEL DEVELOPMENT. All educational personnel at all professional and non-professional levels should be provided continuous pre-service and in-service programs at the local, city, State, and Federal levels. Programs should stress: acquisition of appropriate attitudes for working with target populations; preparation for process-centered learning; utilization of life experiences of students; techniques for involving community residents; cooperative work with supportive services staffing; and flexible use of traditional and non-traditional educational settings. Basic reform in personnel development must occur in three areas: recruitment, training programs and staff development.

3. CURRICULUM. Curriculum is defined as a clearly articulated master plan for the educative process which includes student-oriented performance objectives; sequenced sets of experiences organized from task analyses; basic strategies for acquiring the knowledge skills and attitudes in these sequences; and evaluation based on the objectives. In addition to traditional academic areas must be curriculum designed to teach the urban child how to cope wih specific urban problems. Special emphasis should be given to the communication processes; and within these, reading should be stressed because of its significance to educational achievement and employment.

4. SUPPORTIVE SERVICES. Such services, adequately staffed, which make effective learning possible, e.g., medical, dental, nutritional, clothing, shelter, social and psychological, counseling and guidance, occupational and educational placement, drop-out prevention, personnel recruitment, and recreational, must be provided the students and their communities.

5. COMMUNITY DETERMINATION. The master plan should provide mechanisms to include the target community with all its human and institutional components, all of which can profit education locally. Such components are the inner city residents, colleges, universities, vocational and technical training institutions, and local private industries and foundations. Of special importance is the contribution which inner city residents can—and should—make.

6. EXPERIMENTATION. This component will serve to try out new concepts, techniques, personnel training, staffing patterns, class organization, etc. Related are those alternative education programs which may be piloted or demonstrated as "sub-programs" in the over-all master plan.

7. ASSESSMENT. This component is defined as the planning and implementation of a design which will determine the extent to which the students in the educational program are manifesting those behaviors stated in its objectives at various educational levels so that necessary modifications and/or redesign of operating programs can occur at a national thrust.

8. FACILITIES. Facilities should be created to use space imaginatively in a manner which integrates them with the local program. Where possible they should afford multipurpose usage and have favorable impact upon local economy and community use.

A minority view held that the Federal government had no appropriate role in the area of recommending criteria and program components.

Need for alternatives to the master plan. Alternative programs outside of or in competition with the master plan should be funded to meet specific needs and problems not taken into account by the more comprehensive master plan. Among alternatives discussed here are educational parks, publicly funded private schools; city-as-classroom structures, etc., as well as the controversial voucher system. Minority viewpoints are also presented.

CHAPTER 9: AN URBAN EDUCATION
ACT—THE AUTHORITY STRUCTURE

The Task Force recommends that the Office of Education, in its development of an Urban Education Act, consider the restructuring of authority on Federal, State, municipal, and community levels—as it applies both to grantor and grantee. New roles must be conceived at each level and are reflected in the four sections of the chapter dealing with the community, the metropolitan area, the State, and the Office of Education.

Rationale for an expanded community role. The Task Force supports the principle that heretofore excluded parents and local community residents must be included in the process of decision-making for the schools if effective changes in urban education are to be achieved. Any new legislation should ensure that the community can develop its own mechanism for significant inclusion; make provision for the training of administrators to accommodate themselves to that mechanism; provide funds for such development and training; and provide for Federal evaluation of institutional change and local evaluation of the mechanism's effectiveness in achieving its obejctive of increased institutional accountability.

The role of the community must be expanded in part because of the relative failures of school boards, school administrators, and teacher organizations to meet local educational needs. In addition, the community has a legitimate role in educational decision-making on the basis of American tradition and their ability to make valid contributions.

This report describes some of the efforts of urban systems to link decision-making authority to the community. Decentralization is discussed in its gradations of the delegation of certain kinds of authority and responsibility by a duly constituted legal school board to a subdivision or unit within its purview. Community determination is discussed in terms of degree: participation in the system; partnership with the system; and control over some school or sub-system within the system.

A majority of the Task Force recommends that decentralization and community determination must be considered as major avenues to institutional change while a minority held that Federal policy in this area was unnecessary.

Relationships among communities in urban areas. While the

main thrust of new legislation should be directed at the inner city with authority for such programs vested in school districts and local communities, the Task Force recommends that an alternative thrust be considered which will involve the larger metropolitan population as participants in an urban education program. Comprehensive metropolitan planning should be encouraged where it will result in: a realignment of present school systems; mutual benefit among education and related agencies; a capitalization on the strengths of an entire metropolitan area in order to meet its needs; a trend toward decentralization of programmatic and administrative matters to individual schools.

This recommendation is based on: the existence of non-localized educational and related problems; the presence of disadvantaged populations outside the central city; a broader potential of pool resources; potential advantages for students through enriched programs; the need for comprehensive educational planning; the existence of scattered successful examples of metropolitan planning; and the compatibility of metropolitanism and decentralization.

Role of the states. An Urban Education Act should clearly define the role of the states, considering both their present practices which often do not favor urban education and their significance for future urban education. The Task Force recommends that the requirements for recognition and correction of inequities in State aid formulas which discriminate against urban areas must be defined. Moreover, the Task Force recommends that the Act provide incentive grants to states which require State matching and State maintenance of effort for the new and improved education programs for the urban impoverished groups.

In addition, incentive funds should be used for: providing for a reform of State school finance programs; establishing urban education units in State departments; revising requirements for certification to permit new sources of personnel; examining and setting standards for physical facilities; creating State and local units for disseminating information about urban educational needs; and creating approval mechanisms for urban education proposals.

Need for Federal reorganization and the establishment of a Bureau of Urban Education. The Task Force recommends the following Office of Education reorganization steps:

1. An interim measure, prior to the passage of an Urban Education Act: the consolidation within the Office of Education of those special programs which serve the needs of disadvantaged children under an Associate Commissioner for Programs Serving the Disadvantaged. An appropriate bureau or office title may be designed in keeping with the current reorganization.

2. As the development of new program authorization permits, the creation of a new Bureau for Urban Education with a clear mandate to operate programs and establish Office-wide priorities to meet effectively and rapidly urban education needs in all Office of Education programs.

Such an office described in (1) above should be afforded priority commensurate with the vital functions it will perform. It should have immediate operating responsibility for programs for the disadvantaged including Title I of ESEA, Follow-Through, Bilingual and Drop-out Prevention programs, and the demonstration project in Anacostia (D.C.). The unit should have its own program, salaries, and expense budget. Staff should be recruited from both Federal and non-Federal sources to reflect a wide range of competencies pertinent to urban programs, legislation, and the like.

The need for such an office is validated by the unsatisfactory efforts of smaller units and special assistant positions to fulfill those functions in the past.

The functions of the new office should include: implementation of the short-term recommendations in this report; coordination of Office of Education efforts to supply materials to Congress pertinent to the passage of the Act; coordination of existing programs which focus on urban areas; administration of those operating programs now authorized by ESEA (Title I, VII, and Section 807); administration of demonstration programs; development and operation of an information center; provision of assistance to local agencies; coordination with other Federal agencies in the development of urban programs; sponsoring programs to keep Federal personnel informed in these areas; assisting the Commissioner in articulating his concerns over urban schools to the public and to Congress.

With the passage of the Act, a Bureau of Urban Education should be created, as described in (2) above, to continue the functions of the office described above, and to implement the new approach to Federal aid to urban schools embodied in the Act. Such a Bureau should be headed by an Associate Commissioner who reports directly to the Commissioner. Its budget should be submitted to the Congress as an entirely distinct line item.

Chapter 10: An Urban Education Act—the Process

A set of principles was developed as guidelines for establishing priorities, eligibility, and facilitating mechanisms for the funding process related to an Urban Education Act. These principles stem from the basic premise that a more than equal educational opportunity is necessary for the inner city student. They are designed to focus Federal effort on a priority basis to those places where equal educational opportunity is farthest from reality. The principles summarized are as follows:

1. Education districts representing the largest eligible urban areas should receive priority in Federal funding.

2. Determination of eligibility of urban areas should be based on economic and performance criteria.

3. Each qualifying area should receive full funds for its program and where sufficient funds are unavailable for full funding of every qualifying urban area in its particular size group, a system of competition for a fully funded grant should be developed.

4. Federal aid should be awarded on a basis that enables maximum feasible eligibility for participation among groups, agencies, and institutions within designated urban areas .(The Task Force recommends that a percentage—5–15 percent—of the funds of the Act be set aside for use by the Commissioner to fund groups other than the regular school authorities which design viable specific experiments for use in the inner city and the other depressed areas in the metropolitan area.)

5. Funding procedures should include a system of regulating recurrent eligibility, with grants renewed on the basis of evidence of quality student performance.

6. The legislation should permit a by-pass of State educational agencies where necessary to achieve urban priority. (Such cases might occur where State educational agencies fail to provide sufficient guarantees of their efficiency and willingness to perform in the capacity of advocates for approval and renewal of urban education programs.)

7. The legislation should permit the participation of non-public school children in the program in ways to introduce a new child services concept of the disadvantaged.

8. Advance funding should be provided for the urban education grants.

9. There should be provision for the phasing in of existing categorical grant programs in the sense of incorporating them into the new urban education mandate.

Chapter 11: An Urban Education Act—the Cost

The Task Force has developed a suggested financial mechanism through which to channel critically needed increased educational resources into the cities. The mechanism which best meets urban educational needs is a formula that will provide an addition of at least a third in educational *resources*: equipment, teachers, counselors, curriculum planning, etc. It is estimated that in terms of an increment to current local educational *expenditures*, a one-third addition to resources will require at least a 50 percent addition to current local educational expenditures.

For the 10,500,000 school children in cities with populations over 100,000, the cost would be $5 billion. If the program were extended to reach children in all cities over 50,000, an additional 4 million students would be included, adding $2 billion more to the cost, totaling an additional $7 billion. Such figures assume a necessary increase of $500.00 per student.

For 1971–72, the Task Force recommends a total expenditure for cities over 100,000 population of $470,200,000 for planning, developmental, and operational grants, including facilities and educational training. By 1975, the expenditure should reach $7,566,000,000.

The cost for including cities of populations over 50,000 in 1971–72 would be an additional $182,100,000 and by 1975, an additional $3,627,000,000. If all three categories of cities are included beginning in FY 1971–72, the initial cost would be $706,900,000 which would rise to $14,541,800,000 in FY 1975.

A minority viewpoint recommends supplemental Federal funding of all school districts at the annual level of $30 million on a formula basis to improve education for all children.

Chapter 12: Short-Term Recommendation for Urban Education

While action on the long-term recommendations above should begin immediately, their full implementation may not be realized for several years. In the interim, there is a critical need for immediate action in the field of urban education. Thus, the Task Force recommends the following short-term measures, based largely on existing legislation and programs noted below, which should be implemented within the next fiscal year or two.

Title I, Elementary and Secondary Educational Act

1. Title I must be funded at or near full authorization.
2. States should be encouraged to concentrate funds in areas with high concentrations of disadvantaged populations.
3. Appropriations must be made in advance.
4. A by-pass amendment should be included to directly aid non-public schools when states fail to do so.
5. HEW audits of local and State administration of Title I funds and other related programs should be made available to the public.

Vocational Education

1. Congress should adequately fund all parts of the Vocational Education Amendments of 1968.
2. The Commissioner should concentrate funds under the discretionary parts of the Vocational Education Amendment on the urban disadvantaged.

Research and Development

1. Top priority should be given to the needs of the urban disadvantaged child.
2. Emphasis should be on developing models which could be used in inner city classrooms across the country.
3. Educational laboratories and Research and Development Centers should focus on urban problems.
4. There should be an effort to involve a broader range of people in the research effort.

Training

1. There should be more effort to bring new kinds of people into the field of education, and to establish early recruitment of such people.

2. The Teacher Corps and the Urban Teacher Corps should be expanded.

3. Challenges in certification laws should be encouraged.

Higher Education

1. There should be fuller funding of existing programs designed to aid the disadvantaged, such as Upward Bound, Special Services, Talent Search, Equal Opportunity grants, work-study, and National Defense Education Act loans.

2. Funds should be made available for one-year federally funded college preparatory programs for the disadvantaged.

Discretionary Funds of the Commissioner

1. Discretionary programs should focus on urban education.

2. New monies should be set aside for planning and instituting urban education programs.

Data on Urban Education Funds

1. Data on the flow of Federal funds to the central city school districts in each Standard Metropolitan Statistical Area should be published annually.

National Commission

1. A National Commission on the Future Financing of American Education should be established.

National Advisory Council

1. Greater weight should be given to the inclusion of poor people on the Council.

2. The Council should be given a clear mandate to review all Federal programs which affect the lives of the disadvantaged.

Rural Areas

While the Task Force feels that urban needs deserve priority consideration and separate treatment, the needs of rural areas deserve comparable study and consideration.

Bibliographical Essay

BIBLIOGRAPHICAL ESSAY

Since the enactment of the Economic Opportunity Act in 1964, American society has been preoccupied with poverty, and a good share of this concern has been directed to the urban slum school and the deprived[1] children whom it serves. A vast literature on the children of the poor and their schools has emerged, and, in the main, it has been concerned with the contemporary urban milieu. In a broad sense, an American society which is multi-racial, ethnically variegated, and socially heterogeneous in its very origins, is a society which has dealt, since its beginnings, with the minority child whatever the anchorage of his minority status. If the term "minority child" is used, and the social context is one of deprivation (whatever form it takes,*viz.*, ghettoization; segregated schools; cultural assault and enforced change, etc.), the term may be enlarged to comprehend the urban black in-migrant poor; Puerto Rican migrants to mainland cities; the Mexican American poor of the Southwest; the economically displaced white poor (the euphemism is "Appalachian poor"); reservation Indians, and migrant Indians; the ethnic poor who reflect relaxed immigration quotas; the agricultural seasonally-employed poor caught in migrancy and rootlessness; and, in the broad historical sense, the ethnic poor of other eras.[2]

[1] Our age has fashioned a constellation of euphemisms to characterize the children of the poor: if "deprived" or "disadvantaged" are most often encountered, they are no less awkward than "culturally deprived," "slow learners," or others which have been in use. See Helen E. Rees, *Deprivation and Compensatory Education* (Boston: Houghton Mifflin, 1968), pp. 8–9. See also, F. Cordasco, "Charles Loring Brace and the Dangerous Classes: Historical Analogues of the Urban Black Poor," *Kansas Journal of Sociology*, Vol. 7 (Winter 1971), pp. 142–147.

[2] Generally, the American poor of other eras have not been adequately studied, and the study of the education of the children of the poor has been neglected by American historians, until very recently (*cf.*, in this regard, the English studies of Victorian poverty and 19th Century

This bibliography is a guide to selected references dealing with the education of the children of the poor. Although the entries have been arranged under five main categories (Role of the School; Dropouts and Delinquency; Characteristics of the Disadvantaged Student; Teaching and Teacher Education; Programs and Materials), the categories, themselves, are very flexibly defined and many of the entries could have been planced in more than one category.

SOCIO-ECONOMIC CONDITIONS OF THE DISADVANTAGED

In dealing with the education of the poor, inevitable attention must be given to a whole range of problems which are implicit in poverty; to unemployment, housing and the ghetto; to race and segregation; to life-styles and family patterns; and to the very ethos which is poverty itself. Many of the entries in the bibliography deal with these phenomena but those materials which deal with them exclusively, and do not have the school as their main concern have been excluded. However, some basic

---

society, e.g., Charles Booth, Life and Labour of the People in London, 3rd ed., London: Macmillan, 1902–03, 17 vols. [Selections from this vast work are in Albert Fried and Richard M. Elman, Charles Booth's London, New York: Pantheon, 1968]; and the earlier Henry Mayhew, London Labour and the London Poor, London: Griffin, Bohn, 1861–62. 4 vols.) See Francesco Cordasco, ed., Jacob Riis Revisited: Poverty and the Slum in Another Era (New York: Doubleday, 1968); and Robert H. Bremner, From the Depths: The Discovery of Poverty in the United States (New York: New York University Press, 1956). Lawrence Cremin's The Transformation of the School (New York: Alfred A. Knopf, 1961) is a good introduction to the history of the American school and the poor (en passant, in its study of the Progressive Movement); and Sol Cohen's Progressives and Urban School Reform (Bureau of Publications, Teachers College, Columbia University, 1964) is an invaluable study of the Public Education Association of New York City, the dynamics of urban poverty, and social reform. See also William W. Brickman, "Notes on the Education of the Poor in Historical and International Perspective," McGill Journal of Education, vol. 3 (Fall 1968), pp. 141–150, which in many ways defines the perimeters of the vast areas of deprivation and the school which await study. For a corpus of texts for late 19th and early 20th century urban poverty, see F. Cordasco, ed., The Social History of Poverty: The Urban Experience. 15 vols. (New York: Garrett Press, 1969–70); and F. Cordasco, ed., Poverty: Sources for the Study of Economic Inequality and its Social Consequences (New York Augustus M. Kelley, 1971), which is a collection of some 100 volumes.

references to poverty, and the socio-economic correlates which are the fabric of deprivation (beyond what is found tangentially in the bibliography's entries) are pulled together here for general reference.

One of the best and most incisive commentaries, in a huge literature on poverty, is Thomas Gladwin, *Poverty: U.S.A.* (Boston: Little, Brown, 1967);[3] and further reference can be made to Sidney Lens, *Poverty-America's Enduring Paradox* (New York: Crowell, 1969); to Henry P. Miller, *Poverty American Style* (Belmont, California: Wadsworth, 1966); to Daniel P. Moynihan, ed., *On Understanding Poverty* (New York: Basic Books, 1969); and to James L. Sundquist, ed., *On Fighting Poverty* (New York: Basic Books, 1969).

To these should be added, Frank Riessman, *Strategies Against Poverty* (New York: Random House, 1969); David N. Alloway and Francesco Cordasco, *Minorities in the American City: A Sociological Primer for Educators* (New York: David McKay, 1970); on social class, one of the best references is S. M. Miller and Frank Riessman, *Social Class and Social Policy* (New York: Basic Books, 1968); the phenomenon of social welfare is adequately dealt with in Thomas D. Sherrad, *Social Welfare and Urban Problems* (New York: Columbia University Press, 1968),[4] and in Richard Titmuss, *Commitment to Welfare* (New York: Pantheon Books, 1968), if in very theoretical terms; the social dynamics of the slum are best studied in Gerald D. Suttles, *The Social Order of the Slum: Ethnicity and Territory in the Inner City* (Chicago: University of Chicago Press, 1968); the "culture of poverty" concept is best explored in the studies of Oscar Lewis, *La Vida: A Puerto Rican Family in the Culture of Poverty* (New York: Random House, 1966), and *A Study of Slum Culture: Backgrounds for La Vida* (New York: Random House, 1968), vast portraits of *Kulturpessimismus* and decadence; but a contrary view should be read in F. Cordasco, "Another Face of Poverty: Oscar Lewis' *La Vida*," Phylon; *The*

[3] Special attention should be given to an incisively perceptive commentary (if controversial) on the societal control of the poor in Frances F. Piven and Richard A. Cloward, *Regulating the Poor: The Functions of Public Welfare* (New York: Pantheon Books, 1971).

[4] Of particular value is Daniel P. Moynihan, *The Politics of A Guaranteed Income: The Nixon Administration and the Family Assistance Plan* (New York: Random House, 1973) which is basic reading for the byzantine politics surrounding attempts at welfare reform.

Atlanta University Review of Race & Culture, 29:88–92, Spring, 1968.

The most comprehensive study of ethnicity, the children of a minority and the American school in the context of poverty is Leonard Covello, *The Social Background of the Italo-American School Child: A Study of the Southern Italian Mores and their Effect on the School Situation in Italy and America*, edited and with an Introduction by F. Cordasco (New York: Rowman & Littlefield, 1972). Also, for notices of the education of immigrant minority children, see F. Cordasco, *Italians in the United States: A Bibliography of Reports, Texts, Critical Studies and Related Materials* (New York: Oriole Edition, 1972); and *The Children of Immigrants in Schools. With An Introductory Essay* by F. Cordasco (Metuchen, New Jersey: Scarecrow Reprint Corp., 1970; originally, 1911), 5 vols. The vitality of the *Landsmanschft* (benevolent societies), and the immigrant social service organizations of the immigrant urban ethnic enclaves (*e.g.*, the Educational Alliance; the Henry Street Settlement; the Baron de Hirsch Fund; the Hebrew Immigrant Aid Society) are graphically recreated in Allan Schoener's *Portal to America: The Lower East Side, 1870–1925* (New York: Holt, Rinehart and Winston, 1967); and in Hutchins Hapgood, *The Spirit of the Ghetto*, ed. by Moses Rischin (Cambridge: Harvard University Press, 1967). The mammoth Equality of Educational Opportunity [the Coleman report] (Washington: U.S. Office of Education, 1966) is one of the most important social documents of our time, and should be consulted along with Daniel P. Moynihan, "Sources of Resistance to the *Coleman Report*," *Harvard Educational Review*, vol. 38 (Winter 1968), pp. 23–36; and Frederick Mosteller and Daniel P. Moynihan, eds., *On Equality of Educational Opportunity* (New York: Random House, 1972) which is a reexamination of data on which the Coleman Report findings were based.

Lastly, a serviceable general bibliographical guide to poverty is Freda L. Paltiel, *Poverty: An Annotated Bibliography* (Ottawa: Canadian Welfare Council, 1966); with continuing reference made to *Poverty and Human Resources Abstracts* (The Institute of Labor and Industrial Relations, University of Michigan) which is issued bimonthly and contains review articles, an annotated bibliography, and recent legislative developments related to all aspects of poverty and human resources.

BIBLIOGRAPHICAL AIDS

A main source of bibliographical information on the education of the disadvantaged child is the *IRCD* Bulletin (Informational Retrieval Center on the Disadvantaged [Teachers College, Columbia University]) which is published five times a year by the Center, operated under a contract with U.S. Office of Education Educational Resources Information Center (*ERIC*); a vast resource of 1740 documents (*Selected Documents on the Disadvantaged*) dealing with the special educational needs of the disadvantaged is available from the U.S. Office of Education (*Number and Author Index*, OE 37001); (*Subject Index*, OE 37002). Additionally see F. Cordasco, "Poor Children and Schools," *Choice*, 7:202–212; 335–356, April/May, 1970; and Meyer Weinberg, *The Education of the Minority Child* (Chicago: Integrated Education Associates, 1970) which is a listing of over 10,000 references.

Periodicals which contain bibliographical information include the *Journal of Negro Education; Urban Education;* the *Urban Review;* and *Education And Urban Society.* The NDEA National Institute For Advanced Study In Teaching Disadvantaged Youth (initiated June 1966) has completed two years of study, research, field programs, and dissemination; its *Bulletin/Final Report* (December 1968) should be consulted. A critical review of the literature is available in Bernard Goldstein, Barbara Steinberg and Harry C. Bredemeier, *Low Income Youth in Urban Areas* (New York: Holt, Rinehart and Winston, 1967) which is both a critical exposition of major concerns and a keyed annotated bibliography; and this should be supplemented by H. Helen Randolph, *Urban Education Bibliography: An Annotated Listing* (New York: Center For Urban Education, 1968) which derives from Project TRUE (Hunter College).[5]

Neglected sources of great value are *Master Annotated Bibliography of the Papers of Mobilization For Youth* (New York:

---

[5] A valuable bibliographical guide for higher education is Winnie Bengelsdorf, *Ethnic Studies In Higher Education: State of the Art and Bibliography* (Washington: American Association of State Colleges and Universities, 1972) which identifies and summarizes recent materials on Ethnic Studies in higher education with notices of programs offering minors, majors, and degrees.

Mobilization For Youth, 1965); and Alfred M. Potts, *Knowing and Educating the Disadvantaged: An Annotated Bibliography* (Alamosa, Colorado: Adams State College, 1965). Some value lies in the awkwardly structured Robert E. Booth, *et al.*, *Culturally Disadvantaged* (Detroit: Wayne State University, 1967) which is a comprehensive classified bibliography and a key-word-out-of-context index.

The education of migrants, Mexican Americans, and Indians, has as a principal bibliographical resource the publications of the ERIC Clearinghouse on Rural Education And Small Schools (New Mexico State University), e.g., *Migrant Education: A Selected Bibliography* (Las Cruces, New Mexico: New Mexico State University, 1969); and *Research Abstracts in Rural Education* (*Ibid.*, continuing); and these should be supplemented by the publications of the Southwest Educational Development Laboratory (Austin, Texas) which operates under Title IV of the Elementary and Secondary Education Act.

Bibliography for the Puerto Rican child is found in Gertrude S. Goldberg, "Puerto Rican Migrants on the Mainland of the United States: A Review of the Literature," *IRCD* Bulletin, Vol. IV (January 1968), pp. 1–12; and in F. Cordasco and Eugene Bucchioni, *The Puerto Rican Community and its Children: A Sourcebook for Teachers, Social Workers, and other Professionals* (New York: Scarecrow Press, 1972), pp. 431–460, a comprehensive listing of some 500 entries. Although essentially a critical exposition, some programmatic bibliographical references are in Richard J. Margolis, *The Losers: A Report on Puerto Ricans and the Public Schools* (New York: Aspira, 1968) which chronicles visits to sixteen schools in seven cities. Reference should also be made to F. Cordasco, *et al.*, *Puerto Ricans on the United States Mainland: A Bibliography of Reports, Texts, Critical Studies, and Related Materials* (New York: Roman & Littlefield, 1972).

GUIDES TO PROGRAMS FOR THE DISADVANTAGED

The most comprehensive guide to programs for the disadvantaged is Edmund W. Gordon and Doxey A. Wilkerson, *Compensatory Education For the Disadvantaged* (New York: College Entrance Examination Board, 1966); with further reference made to *Education: An Answer to Poverty* (Washington:

U.S. Office of Education and Office of Economic Opportunity, 1966). Of particular importance are the *Disadvantaged Children Series* published by the U.S. Office of Education: *Educating Disadvantaged Children Under Six* (1965); *Educating Children in the Middle Grades* (1965); *Administration of Elementary School Programs For Disadvantaged Children* (1966); *Educating Disadvantaged Children in the Elementary School: An Annotated Bibliography* (1966). A useful guide to centers of the study of deprivation and compensatory education is Helen E. Rees, "Centers of Study and Sources of Information," *Deprivation and Compensatory Education* (New York: Houghton Mifflin, 1968), pp. 237–260. As to opportunities in higher education for minority students, reference should be made to *A Chance To Go To College: A Directory of 800 Colleges that Have Special Help For Students From Minorities and Low-Income Families* (New York: College Entrance Examination Board, 1971); Gloria Goldstein, *College Bound: A Directory of Special Programs and Financial Aid For Minority Group Students* (White Plains, New York: Urban League of Westchester, 1970); and *A Chance to Learn: An Action Agenda For Equal Opportunity in Higher Education* (Berkeley: Carnegie Commission on Higher Education, 1970).

Bibliographical Register of Titles:

a. Role of the School
b. Dropouts and Delinquency
c. Characteristics of the Disadvantaged Student
d. Teaching and Teacher Education
e. Programs and Materials

ROLE OF THE SCHOOL

1. **Adkins, Arthur.** "Inequities Between Suburban and Urban Schools." *Educational Leadership*, 26:243–245, December 1968. Notes that the inequities between urban and suburban schools are not altogether one-sided.

2. **Bernstein, Abraham.** *The Education of Urban Populations* (New York: Random House, 1967).

3. **Berube, Maurice R.** "White Liberals, Black Schools." *Commonweal*, 85:71–73, October 21, 1966.

4. **Berube, Maurice R.** and **Marilyn Gittell.** *Confrontation at Ocean Hill-Brownsville: The New York School Strikes of 1968* (New York: Frederick A. Praeger, 1969).

5. **Bloom, Benjamin S.** *Compensatory Education for Cultural Deprivation* (New York: Holt, Rinehart & Winston, 1965).

6. **Boardman, Richard P.** "Public and Parochial." *The Urban Review*, 1:16–25, November 1966. Proposes that the presence of parallel education systems in an urban area has consequences for the form and quality of educational services in that area.

7. **Brameld, Theodore.** *Cultural Foundations of Education: An Interdisciplinary Exploration* (New York: Harper, 1957).

8. **Brameld, Theodore.** *The Use of Explosive Ideas in Education: Culture, Class, and Evolution* (Pittsburgh: University of Pittsburgh Press, 1965).

9. **Brickman, William W.** and **Stanley Lehrer,** eds. *The Countdown on Segregated Education* (New York: Society for the Advancement of Education, 1960).

10. **Brickman, William W.** and **Stanley Lehrer,** eds., *Education and the Many Faces of the Disadvantaged: Cultural and Historical Perspectives* (New York: John Wiley, 1972).

11. **Brooke, Edward W.** "Crisis in the Cities." *Pennsylvania School Journal*, 116:308 ff., February 1968. Discussion concerning poverty.

12. **Burgess, Evangeline.** *Values in Early Childhood Education*, 2d ed. (Washington: National Education Association, 1965).

13. **Chandler, B. J.** *Education in Urban Society* (New York: Dodd, Mead, 1962).

14. **Clark, Harold F.** and **Harold S. Stone.** *Classrooms on Main Street* (New York: Teachers College Press, 1966).

15. **Clift, Virgil A.** "Factors Relating to the Education of Culturally Deprived Negro Youth," *Educational Theory*, 14:76–82, April, 1964.

16. **Clift, Virgil A.,** ed., *Negro Education in America: Its Adequacy, Problems, and Needs* (New York: Harper, 1962).

17. **Clinchy, Evans.** "Good School in a Ghetto." *Saturday Review*, November 16, 1968, pp. 106 ff. Boston's Boardman Elementary School which is in a Roxbury urban renewal area.

18. **Cohen, David K.** "Policy for Public Schools: Compensation and Integration." *Harvard Educational Review*, 38:114–137, Winter 1968. Changes advocated for urban education, with the focus upon those few basic aspects of urban public education which could be fundamentally changed by the limited instruments of national policy.

19. **Coleman, James S.,** and others. *Equality of Educational Opportunity and Supplemental Appendix. . . .* (Washington: U.S. Office of Education, 1966). 2v.

20. **Commission on School Integration.** *Public School Segregation and Integration in the North* (Washington: National Association for Intergroup Relations Officials, 1963).

21. **[Community Education]** "Community Education: A Special Issue," *Phi Delta Kappan*, 54:146–224, November 1972.

22. **Conant, James Bryant.** *Slums and Suburbs: A Commentary on Schools in Metropolitan Areas.* (New York: McGraw-Hill, 1961).

23. Conference on Integration in the New York City Public Schools, Columbia University, 1963. *Integrating the Urban School: Proceedings* (New York: Bureau of Publications, Teachers College, Columbia University, 1963).

24. **Cordasco, Francesco.** "A Quartet of Volumes Preoccupied with Poverty," *Phi Delta Kappan*, 54:354–355, January 1973. Critique-essay on urban education.

25. **Cordasco, Francesco.** "Educational Pelagianism: The Schools and the Poor," *Teachers College Record*, 69:705–709, April, 1968.

26. **Cordasco, Francesco; Maurie Hillson;** and **Henry A. Bullock.** *The School In the Social Order: A Sociological Introduction to Educational Understanding* (Scranton: International Textbook Co., 1970).

27. **Corwin, Ronald G.** *A Sociology of Education: Emerging Patterns of Class, Status, and Power in the Public Schools* (New York: Appleton-Century-Crofts, 1965).

28. **Cowles, Milly.** *Perspectives in the Education of Disadvantaged Children* (Cleveland: World Publishing Co., 1967).

29. **Cronin, Joseph M.** *The Control of Urban Schools: Perspectives on Power* (New York: The Free Press, 1972).

30. **Cuban, Larry.** "Urban schools and the Negro." *Social Education*, 31:478–482, October 1967.

31. **Crain, Robert L.** *The Politics of School Desegregation* (Chicago: Aldine Publishing Co., 1968).

32. **Crossland, Fred E.** *Minority Access to College* (New York: Schocken, 1971).

33. **Crow, Lester Donald; Walter J. Murray;** and **Hugh Smythe.** *Educating the Culturally Disadvantaged Child: Principles and Programs* (New York: D. McKay Co., 1966).

34. **Decter, Midge.** "The Negro and the New York Schools," *Commentary*, 38:25–34, September, 1964.

35. **Demak, Leonard S.** "Impact of Social Forces on Public Schools in Cities." *Educational Leadership*, 26:177–185, November 1968.

36. **Edgar, Earl E.** *Social Foundations of Education* (New York: Center for Applied Research in Education, 1965).

37. "Education in the Ghetto." *Saturday Review*, January 11, 1969, pp. 33–61. A special section which contains several articles concerned with solution to the problems of education in the ghetto. The contributors include Theodore R. Sizer, Alan K. Campbell, Kenneth W. Haskins, and Albert Shanker.

38. "Education for Socially Disadvantaged Children," *Review of Educational Research*, 35:375–426, December, 1965.

39. **Educational Policies Commission.** *American Education and the Search for Equal Opportunity* (Washington: National Education Association, 1965).

40. **Educational Policies Commission.** *Education and the Disadvantaged American* (Washington: National Educational Association, 1962).

41. **Estes, Nolan.** "Answers for the Inner City." *Pennsylvania School Journal*, 117:92–95, October 1968. Emphasizes the need for a better understanding of the nature of poverty and racial isolation in our central cities.

42. [Ethnic Education] "The Imperatives of Ethnic Education," *Phi Delta Kappan*, 53:265–343, January 1972. Multi-ethnic schools; Chicano children; White ethnics; Blacks; Puerto Ricans.

43. Everett, John R. "The Decentralization Fiasco and Our Ghetto Schools." *Atlantic Monthly*, 222:71–73, December 1968.

44. Fantini, Mario and Gerald Weinstein. *The Disadvantaged: Challenge To Education* (New York: Harper & Row, 1968).

45. Featherstone, Richard L. and Frederick W. Hill. "Urban School Decentralization; Part I, The Bundy Report: What it Really Means." *American School and University*, 41:44 ff, October 1968.

46. Ferrer, Terry. *The Schools and Urban Renewal: A Case Study from New Haven* (New York: Educational Facilities Laboratories, 1964).

47. "Five Big-city Districts Fight to Come Back." *School Management*, 12:38 ff, June 1968. Philadelphia, Seattle, Milwaukee, Denver, and San Francisco.

48. Friedenberg, Edgar. "Requiem for the Urban School," *Saturday Review*, 50:77–79; 92–94, November 1967.

49. Frierson, Edward C. "Determining Needs," *Education*, 85:461–466, April, 1965.

50. Frost, Joe L. and Glenn R. Hawkes, eds. *The Disadvantaged Child: Issues and Innovations* (Boston: Houghton Mifflin, 1966). 2nd ed., 1970.

51. Fuchs, Estelle. *Pickets at the Gates* (New York: Free Press, 1966).

52. Furness, W. Todd. *Higher Education for Everybody?* (Washington: American Council on Education, 1971).

53. Giles, Hermann Harry. *The Integrated Classroom* (New York: Basic Books, 1959).

54. Ginsburg, H. *The Myth of the Deprived Child* (Englewood Cliffs: Prentice Hall, 1972).

55. **Gittell, Marilyn.** *Participants and Participation: A Study of School Policy in New York City* (New York: Praeger, 1967).

56. **Gittell, Marilyn** and **T. Edward Hollander.** *Six Urban School Districts: A Comparative Study of Institutional Response* (New York: Praeger, 1968). Concerned with Baltimore, Chicago, Detroit, New York, Philadelphia, and St. Louis.

57. **Gold, Stephen F.** "School-community Relations in Urban Ghettos." *Teachers College Record*, 69:145–150, November 1967. Emphasizes the need for understanding the ways in which schools and teachers are perceived by the poor, the way in which status and class differentials impede interaction, and the resentment aroused when teachers concentrate mainly upon "control."

58. **Gordon, Ira J.** *Parent Involvement in Compensatory Education* (Urbana, Illinois: University of Illinois Press, 1971).

59. **Graubard, Allen.** *Free the Children: Radical Reform and the Free School Movement* (New York: Pantheon, 1972).

60. **Greene, Mary Frances** and **Orletta Ryan.** *The School Children Growing Up in The Slums* (New York: Pantheon Books, 1965).

61. **Halpern, Ray** and **Betty Halpern.** "The City That Went to School: Integration in Berkeley." *The Nation*, 206: 632–636, May 13, 1968.

62. **Harrison, Bennett.** *Education, Training, and the Urban Ghetto* (Baltimore: Johns Hopkins University Press, 1972). Three year study of workers in 16 cities.

63. **Havighurst, Robert J.** and **Daniel U. Levine.** *Education in Metropolitan Areas*, 2nd Ed. (Boston: Allyn & Bacon, 1971).

64. **Havighurst, Robert J.** "The Educationally Difficult Student: What the Schools Can Do," *Bulletin Of National*

Association of Secondary School Principals, 41:110–27, March, 1965.

65. **Hawes, Joseph M.** *Children in Urban Society: Juvenile Delinquency in 19th Century America* (New York: Oxford University Press, 1971).

66. **Heidenreich, Richard,** ed. *Urban Education* (New York: College Readings, 1972).

67. **Hellmuth, Jerome,** ed. *Disadvantaged Child* (New York: Brunner/Mazel, 1969–1970). 3 vols.

68. **Henderson, George.** "School-Community Relations in Poverty Areas." *Peabody Journal of Education*, 45: 209–213, January 1968.

69. **Herriott, Robert E.** and **Nancy Hoyt St. John.** *Social Class and the Urban School: The Impact of Pupil Background on Teachers and Principals* (New York: Wiley, 1966).

70. **Hickerson, Nathaniel.** *Education for Alienation* (New York: Prentice-Hall, 1966).

71. **Hillson, Maurie; Francesco Cordasco;** and **Francis P. Purcell.** *Education and the Urban Community: Schools and the Crisis of the Cities* (New York: American Book Co., 1969).

72. **Howe, Harold.** "First Rate Cities, First Rate Schools." *National Elementary Principal*, 47:38–42, September 1967.

73. **Hummel, Raymond C.** *Urban Education in America: Problems and Prospects* (New York: Oxford University Press, 1973).

74. **Hunnicutt, Clarence W.** *Urban Education and Cultural Deprivation* (Syracuse: Syracuse University, 1964).

75. "Indian Education," *Research Abstracts in Rural Education* [New Mexico State University, January, 1969], pp. 30–37.

76. [Indian Education] Wolcott, Harry F. *A Kwakiutl Village and School* (New York: Holt, Rinehart & Winston, 1967).

77. **Jackson, Ronald B.** "Schools and Communities: A Necessary Relevance," *Clearing House*, 44:488–490, 1970.

78. **Jacoby, Susan L.** "Big City Schools—Washington: National Monument to Failure," *Saturday Review of Literature*, 50:71–73; 89–91, November 1967.

79. **Jacoby, Susan L.** "The Making of a Community School." *The Urban Review*, 2:3–4, February 1968.

80. **Jaffa, N. Neubert** and **Richard M. Brandt.** "An Approach to the Problems of a Downtown School." *National Elementary Principal*, 44:25–28, November 1964.

81. **Jaffe, A. J.; Walter Adams;** and **Sandra G. Meyers.** *Negro Higher Education In the 1960's* (New York: Praeger, 1968).

82. **Janowitz, Morris.** *Institution Building in Urban Education* (New York: Russell Sage Foundation, 1970).

83. **Jencks, Christopher,** et al. *Inequality: A Reassessment of the Effect of Family* and Schooling in America (New York: Basic Books, 1972). A three year study, conducted at the Harvard Center for Educational Policy Research. See Godfrey Hodgson, "Do Schools Make A Difference," *Atlantic*, March 1973, pp. 35–36.

84. **Kaplan, B. A.** "Issues in Educating the Culturally Disadvantaged," *Phi Delta Kappan*, 45:70–6, November, 1963.

85. **Karp, Richard.** "School Decentralization in New York: A Case Study." *Interplay*, 11:9–14, August–September 1968. Concerned with community control of public schools.

86. **Katz, Michael.** *Class, Bureaucracy and Schools: The Illusion of Educational Change in America* (New York: Praeger, 1971).

87. **Katzman, Martin.** "The Burdens on Big City Schools." *Urban Education*, 111:112–123, 1967. "In this brief essay, I hope to clarify the problems of big city schools as seen by an economist. The aim is to distinguish problems common to providing any public service, to providing schooling, and to providing schooling in a big city."

88. **Katzman, Martin T.** *The Political Economy of Urban Schools* (Cambridge: Harvard University Press, 1971). Fifty-six elementary school districts in Boston.

89. **Kennedy, Robert F.,** et al. "Ghetto Education." *The Center Magazine*, 1:45–60, November 1968.

90. **Kerber, August** and **Wilfred R. Smith,** eds. *Educational Issues in a Changing Society* (Detroit: Wayne State University Press, 1964).

91. **Kerber, August** and **Barbara Bommarito,** eds. *The Schools and the Urban Crisis: A Book of Readings* (New York: Holt, Rinehart and Winston, 1965).

92. **Kerckhoff, R. K.** "Problem of the City School," *Journal of Marriage and the Family*, 26:435–9, November, 1964.

93. **Knapp, Robert B.** *Social Integration in Urban Communities: A Guide for Educational Planning* (New York: Bureau of Publications, Teachers College, Columbia University, 1960).

94. **Kohl, Herbert.** "Integrate with Whom?" *Interplay*, 11:27 ff., June–July 1968. Concerned with the "failure" of integration as an educational policy.

95. **Kozol, Jonathan.** "Alienation or Interaction?" *NEA Journal*, 57:48 ff. Emphasizes the need for the maximum possible interaction between the school and its community.

96. **Kozol, Jonathan.** "Let the Ghetto Run Its Own Schools." *Saturday Evening Post*, 241:10–14, June 1, 1968.

97. **Kvaraceus, W. C.** "Social Stresses and Strains on Children and Youth: Some Implications for Schools," *High School Journal*, 47:140–5, January, 1964.

98. **Landes, Ruth.** *Culture in American Education: Anthropological Approaches to Minority and Dominant Groups in the Schools* (New York: Wiley, 1965).

99. **Lauter, Paul** and **Florence Howe.** "The School Mess." *New York Review of Books*, X:16–21, January 18, 1968.

100. **Lazerson, Marvin.** *Origins of the Urban School: Public Education in Massachusetts, 1870–1915* (Cambridge: Harvard University Press, 1971).

101. **Levin, Henry M.,** ed. *Community Control of Schools* (Washington: Brookings Institution, 1970).

102. **Levine. Daniel U.** "The Community School in Historical Perspective," *Elementary School Journal*, 67:192–195, 1967.

103. **Levine, Daniel U.** "The Integration-Compensatory Education Controversy." *Educational Forum*, 32:323–332. March 1968. The contradictions inherent in the efforts to eliminate the segregated patterns of schooling in cities and to organize special remedial programs that might compensate for the learning handicaps associated with a background of deprivation and poverty.

104. **Levine, Daniel U.** "Integration: Reconstructing Academic Values of Youths in Deprived Areas," *Clearing House*, 39:159-162, November, 1964.

105. **Levine, L. S.** "Imposed Social Position, Assessment and Curricular Implications," *Bulletin of National Association of Secondary School Principals*, 50:44–74, May, 1966.

106. **Lewis, Gertrude M.** and **Esther Murow.** *Educating Disadvantaged Children* in the Elementary School. (Disadvantaged Children Series, no. 5) (Washington: U.S. Office of Education, 1966).

107. **Loretan, J. O.** "Problems in Improving Educational Opportunities for Puerto Ricans in New York. Third Annual Conference for New Yorkers of Puerto Rican Background," *High Points*, 45:23–31, May, 1963.

108. **McKendall, B. W., Jr.** "Breaking the Barriers of Cultural Disadvantage and Curriculum Imbalance," *Phi Delta Kappan*, 46:307–11, March, 1965.

109. **MacKintosh, Helen K.; Lillian Gore;** and **Gertrude M. Lewis.** *Educating Disadvantaged Children Under Six.* Disadvantaged Children Series, no. 1. (Washington: U.S. Office of Education, 1966).

110. **MacKintosh, Helen K.; Lillan Gore;** and **Gertrude M. Lewis.** *Educating Disadvantaged Children in the Middle Grades.* Disadvantaged Children Series, no. 3. (Washington: U.S. Office of Education, 1965).

111. **MacKintosh, Helen K.; Lillian Gore;** and **Gertrude M. Lewis.** *Educating Disadvantaged Children in the Primary Years.* Disadvantaged Children Series, no. 2. (Washington: U.S. Office of Education, 1965).

112. **Maher, Terrance P.,** ed. *Challenge to Education: Teaching the Disadvantaged* (New York: Praeger, 1971). 3 vols.

113. **Marburger, Carl.** "Educational Problems of Culturally Deprived Children and Youth," in Mahar, Mary H. *School Library Supervision in Large Cities* (Washington: U.S. Office of Education, 1966), pp. 25–35.

114. **Marcus, Sheldon** and **Philip D. Vairo,** eds. *Urban Education: Crisis or Opportunity?* (Metuchen, N.J.: Scarecrow Press, 1972).

115. **Mays, John Barron.** *Education and the Urban Child* (Liverpool: Liverpool University Press, 1962).

116. **Miller, Henry L.,** ed. *Education for the Disadvantaged* (New York: Macmillan-Free Press, 1967).

117. **National Conference on Education of the Disadvantaged.** *Report* (Washington: United States Department of Health, Education, and Welfare, 1966).

118. **National Education Association.** Department of Elementary, Kindergarten, Nursery Education. *Prevention of Failure* (Washington: National Education Association, 1965).

119. **National Society for the Study of Education.** *The Changing American School.* Pt. 2. Yearbook 1965. (Chicago: University of Chicago, 1966).

120. **National Society for the Study of Education.** Committee on the Educationally Retarded and Disadvantaged. *The Educationally Retarded and Disadvantaged.* Ed. by Paul A. Witty. Pt. 1. Yearbook 1966. (Chicago: University of Chicago Press, 1967).

121. **Nichols, David C.** and **Olive Mills.** *The Campus and the Racial Crisis* (Washington: American Council on Education, 1970).

122. **O'Hara, M.** "We Heighten the Child's Self-Image Through the School: A Selected Bibliography," *High Points,* 48:71–9, June, 1966.

123. **Ornstein, A. C.** "Effective Schools for Disadvantaged Children," *Journal of Secondary Education,* 46:105–9, March, 1965.

124. **Passow, A. Harry,** ed. *Education of the Disadvantaged: A Book of Readings* (New York: Holt, Rinehart and Winston, 1967).

125. **Passow, A. Harry,** ed. *Education in Depressed Areas* (New York: Bureau of Publications, Teachers College, 1963).

126. **Passow, A. Harry.** *Toward Creating a Model Urban School System: A Study of the Washington, D.C. Public Schools* (New York: Teachers College, Columbia University, 1967).

127. **Passow, A. Harry,** ed. *Reaching the Disadvantaged Learner* (New York: Teachers College Press, 1970).

128. **Passow, A. Harry,** ed. *Urban Education in the 1970s* (New York: Teachers College Press, 1971).

129. **Passow, A. Harry,** ed. *Opening Opportunities for Disadvantaged Learners* (New York: Teachers College Press, 1972).

130. **Phi Delta Kappa.** Commission on the Study of Educational Policies and Programs in Relation to Desegregation. *Action Patterns in School Desegregation: A Guidebook* (Bloomington, Ind.: Phi Delta Kappa, 1959).

131. **Piven, Frances Fox** and **Richard A. Cloward.** "The Case Against Urban Desegregation." *Social Work,* 12:12–22, January 1967. For an answer to this article, see Funnye and Shiffman, "The Imperative of Deghettoization: An Answer to Piven and Cloward," *Social Work,* April 1967, pp. 5–11.

132. **Platt, Anthony M.** *The Child Savers: The Invention of Delinquency* (Chicago: University of Chicago Press, 1969).

133. **Pressman, Harvey.** "The Failure of the Public Schools." *Urban Education,* 11:61–81, 1966. An examination of some of the evidence "which indicates the enormity of the failure of the urban public schools to educate the poor in the past and in the present."

134. **Proctor, Samuel.** "Reversing the Spiral Toward Futility," in *Eighteenth Yearbook of the American Association of Colleges for Teacher Education* (Washington: AACTE, 1965).

135. [The] *Puerto Rican Study, 1953–1957. A Report on the Education and Adjustment of Puerto Rican Pupils in the Public Schools of the City of New York* (New York: Board of Education, 1958; reissued with an introduction by F. Cordasco, New York: Oriole Editions, 1972).

136. **Rees, Helen E.** *Deprivation and Compensatory Education: A Consideration* (Boston: Houghton Mifflin, 1968).

137. **Reiss, Albert J.,** ed. *Schools in a Changing Society* (New York: Free Press, 1965).

138. **Renner, Richard R.** "Schools and the Poor: The High Cost of Classroom Candor." *Educational Forum*, 32: 55-63, November 1967.

139. **Rever, Philip R.,** ed. *Open Admissions and Equal Access* (Iowa City, Iowa: American College Testing Program, 1971).

140. **Riese, Hertha Pataky.** *Heal the Hurt Child: An Approach Through Educational Therapy with Special Reference to the Extremely Deprived Negro Child* (Chicago: University of Chicago Press, 1962).

141. **Riles, Wilson C., Chairman.** *The Urban Education Task Force Report. Final Report of the Task Force on Urban Education to the Department of Health, Education, and Welfare* (New York: Praeger, 1970).

142. **Roberts, Joan I.** *School Children in the Urban Slum* (New York: Macmillan, 1967).

143. **Roberts, Wallace.** "The Battle for Urban Schools." *Saturday Review*, November 16, 1968, pp. 97 ff. "The spreading struggle for community control of inner city schools involves a complex of social and political issues —black power, the tenure rights of teachers, black and white racism, and the prerogatives of organized labor."

144. **Rodgers, David.** *110 Livingston Street: Politics and Bureaucracy in the New York City School System* (New York: Random House, 1968).

145. **Rosenthal, Alan,** ed. *Governing Education: A Reader on Politics, Power, and Public School Policy* (New York: Doubleday, 1969).

146. **Rubenstein, Annette T.,** ed. *Schools Against Children: The Case for Community Control* (New York: Monthly Review Press, 1970).

147. **Rudman, Herbert C.** and **R. L. Featherstone,** eds. *Urban Schooling* (New York: Harcourt, Brace and World, 1968).

148. **Salisbury, Robert H.** "Schools and Politics in the Big City." *Harvard Educational Review*, 37:408–424, Summer 1967. Possible relationships between urban political systems and the schools.

149. **Sexton, Patricia Cayo.** *Education and Income: Inequalities of Opportunity in Our Public Schools* (New York: Viking Press, 1961).

150. **Shoben, Edward Joseph, Jr.** "Education in Megalopolis." *Educational* Forum, 31:431–439, May 1967. Problems of developing effective educational systems within the megalopolis.

151. **Smiley, Marjorie B.** and **Harry L. Miller,** eds. *Policy Issues in Urban Education* (New York: Macmillan— The Free Press, 1968).

152. **Solomon, Victor.** "An Independent Board of Education for Harlem." *Urban Affairs Quarterly,* IV: 39–63, September 1968. Suggests that black separatism may be a necessary prelude for assimilation and integration to take place on an egalitarian basis.

153. **Steinberg, E. R.** "Middle-Class Education for Lower-Class Students," *Education,* 86:67–74, October, 1965.

154. **Stone, James C.,** and **DeNevi, Donald P.,** eds. *Teaching Multi-Cultural Populations* (New York: Van Nostrand Reinhold, 1971). (Blacks; Puerto Ricans; Mexicans; Asians; and Indians).

155. **Swanson, Austin D.** "An Analysis of the Fiscal Problems of Large City School Systems." *Urban Education,* I:149–163, 1965. Implications of several studies which have been made concerning fiscal problems of large city school systems.

156. **Swanson, Bert E.** *The Struggle for Equality: School Integration Controversy in New York City* (New York: Hobbs, Dorman and Company, 1966).

157. **Thomas, Robert Murray.** *Social Differences in the Classroom: Social-Class, Ethnic, and Religious Problems* (New York: D. McKay Co., 1965).

158. **Toffler, Alvin,** ed. *The Schoolhouse in the City* (New York, Praeger, 1968). Contributions by Bayard Rustin, Kenneth Clark, Robert Havighurst, and other authoritative writers.

159. [Urban Education] "The Reform of Urban Education," *Phi Delta Kappan*, 52:327–390, February 1971.

160. [Urban Education] "Problems of Urban Education," *Phi Delta Kappan*, 48:305–376, March, 1967.

161. U.S. Commission on Civil Rights. *Racial Isolation in the Public Schools* (Washington: U.S. Government Printing Office, 1967). 2 vols.

162. Vairo, Philip D. and William M. Perel. *Urban Education: Problems and Prospects* (New York: David McKay, 1969).

163. Vontress, Clemont E. "Our Demoralizing Slum Schools," *Phi Delta Kappan*, 45:77–81, November 1963.

164. Weinberg, Meyer. *Integrated Education: A Reader* Beverly Hills, Calif.: Glecoe Press, 1968).

165. Wilcox, Preston R. "The School and the Community." *Teachers College Record*, 69:133–142, November 1967. Develops a contemporary model for the community-centered schools with special reference to minority groups in city slums.

166. Willingham, Warren W. *Free-Access Higher Education* (New York: College Entrance Board, 1970).

167. Wise, Arthur E. *Rich Schools, Poor Schools. The Promise of Equal Educational Opportunity* (Chicago: University of Chicago Press, 1968).

168. Work Conference on Curriculum and Teaching in Depressed Urban Areas, Columbia University, 1962. *Education in Depressed Areas* (New York: Bureau of Publications, Teachers College, Columbia University, 1963). See #125.

169. Zimmer, Basil G. and Amos H. Hawley. "Factors Associated with Resistance to the Organization of Metropolitan Area Schools." *Sociology of Education*, 40:334–347, Fall 1967. Factors which are associated with resistance to the reorganization of school districts in metropolitan areas.

DROPOUTS AND DELINQUENCY

170. [Boston] *The Way We Go To School*. Task Force on Children Out of School. (Boston: Beacon Press, 1971).

171. Cervantes, Lucius F. *The Dropout: Causes and Cures* (Ann Arbor: University of Michigan Press, 1965).

172. Dentler, Robert A. "Dropouts, Automation and the Cities," *Teachers College Record*, 65:475–83, March, 1964.

173. Dentler, Robert A. and Mary E. Warshauer. *Big City Dropouts and Illiterates* (New York: Frederick A. Praeger, 1968).

174. Duncan, B. "Dropouts and the Unemployed," *Journal of Political Economy*, 73:123–34, April, 1965.

175. Elam, Sophie L. "Poverty and Acculturation in A Migrant Puerto Rican Family," *Teachers College Record*, 70:617–23, April, 1969.

176. *Equal Educational Opportunity* [Harvard Educational Review] (Cambridge, Mass.: Harvard University Press, 1969). See #19.

177. Farrow, R. B. "Schools and Help for the Offending Child," *Childhood Education*, 41:123–34, April, 1965.

178. Fleisher, B. M. "Effect of Income on Delinquency," *American Economic Review*, 56:118–37, March, 1966).

179. Glazer, Mona Y. and Carol F. Creedon, eds. *Children and Poverty* (Chicago: Rand McNally, 1968).

180. Gowan, John C. and George D. Demos, eds. *The Disadvantaged and Potential Dropout: Compensatory Educational Programs: A Book of Readings* (Springfield, Ill.: C. C. Thomas, 1966).

181. Henderson, George. "Opportunity and Alienation in Public Schools." *Teachers College Record*, 69:151–157, November 1967. Emphasizes the importance of coun-

tering deviation and alienation by increasing the opportunities for young people to learn the roles acceptable to the dominant culture.

182. *The Juvenile Delinquency Prevention Act of 1967* (Hearings before the General Subcommittee on Education of the Committee on Education and Labor, House of Representatives, 90th Congress, 1st session on H.R. 7642, 1967).

183. **Kelly, F. J.** and others. "Multiple Discriminant, Prediction of Delinquency and School Dropouts," *Educational and Psychological Measurement*, 24:535–44, Fall, 1964.

184. **Liddle, G. P.** "Secondary School as an Instrument for Preventing Juvenile Delinquency," *High School Journal*, 47:146–52, January, 1964.

185. **Mink, Oscar G.** and **Kaplan, B. A.** *America's Problem Youth, Education and Guidance of the Disadvantaged* (Scranton: International Textbook Co., 1970).

186. **Purcell, Francis P.** and **Maurie Hillson.** "The Disadvantaged Child: A Product of the Culture of Poverty, His Education, and His Life Chances," *Eugenics Quarterly*, 13:179–185, September, 1966.

187. **Schreiber, Daniel,** ed. *Guidance and the School Dropout* (Washington: Project: School Dropouts, National Education Association and American Personnel and Guidance Association, 1964).

188. **Schreiber, Daniel,** ed. *The School Dropout* (Washington: Project: School Dropouts, National Education Association, 1964).

189. **Strom, Robert D.** "A Realistic Curriculum for the Predictive Dropout," *Clearing House*, 39:101–106, October, 1964.

190. **Willie, Charles V.** and others. "Race and Delinquency," *Phylon*, 26:240–246, Spring, 1965.

191. **Zirbes, L.** "Dropouts in Long Perspective," *Childhood Education*, 40:345–8, March, 1964.

CHARACTERISTICS OF THE DISADVANTAGED STUDENT

192. **Beymer, L.** "Pros and cons of the National Assessment Project," *Clearing House*, 40:540–3, May, 1966.

193. **Black, Millard H.** "Characteristics of the Culturally Disadvantaged Child," *Reading Teacher*, 18:465–70, March, 1965.

194. **Braithwaite, Edward R.** *To Sir, With Love* (Englewood Cliffs, N.J.: Prentice-Hall, 1962). The story of a Negro teacher in a London slum area.

195. **Brussell, Charles B.** *Disadvantaged Mexican American Children and Early Educational Experience* (Austin, Texas: Southwest Educational Development Corporation, 1968).

196. **Cordasco, Francesco.** "The Challenge of the Non-English Speaking Child in the American School," *School & Society*, 96:198–201, March 30, 1968.

197. **Cordasco, Francesco.** "Puerto Rican Pupils and American Education," *School & Society*, 95:116–119, February 18, 1967.

198. **Cordasco, Francesco.** "Charles Loring Brace and the Dangerous Classes: Historical Analogues of the Urban Black Poor," *Kansas Journal of Sociology*, 7:142–147, Winter 1971. (Notices of "placing out" of poor children.)

199. **Cordasco, Francesco** and **J. Redd.** "Summer Camp Education For Underprivileged Children," *School & Society*, 23:299–300, Summer, 1965.

200. **Cordasco, Francesco** and **Eugene Bucchioni.** *Puerto Rican Children in Mainland Schools: A Sourcebook for Teachers* (New York: Scarecrow Press, 1968). 2nd ed., 1972.

201. **Daniels, V.** "Concerning the Validity of Standardized Tests," *Clearing House,* 39:12–14, September, 1964.

202. **Deutsch, Martin** and others. *The Disadvantaged: Studies of the Social Environment and Learning* (New York: Basic Books, 1967).

203. **Duncan, John B.** and **Albert Mindlin.** "Municipal Fair Housing Legislation: Community Beliefs and Facts," *Phylon,* 25:217–237, Fall, 1964.

204. **Eells, Kenneth Walter.** *Intelligence and Cultural Differences: A Study of Cultural Learning and Problem-Solving* (Chicago: University of Chicago Press, 1951).

205. "Evaluation: Case Studies," *Nation's Schools,* 77:59–66, May, 1966.

206. **Feldmann, S.** and **M. Weiner.** "Use of a Standardized Reading Achievement Test with Two Levels of Socio-Economic Status Pupils," *Journal of Experimental Education,* 32:269–274, Spring, 1964.

207. **Frierson, Edward C.** "Upper and Lower Status Gifted Children: A Study of Differences," *Exceptional Children,* 32:83–90, 1965.

208. **Grebler, Leo; Joan W. Moore;** and **Ralph C. Guzman.** *The Mexican American People: The Nation's Second Largest Minority* (New York: Free Press, 1969).

209. **Green, Robert L.** and **William W. Farquhar.** "Negro Academic Motivation and Scholastic Achievement," *Journal of Educational Psychology,* 56:241–243, October, 1965.

210. **Heller, Celia S.** *Mexican American Youth: Forgotten Youth At the Crossroad* (New York: Random House, 1966).

211. **Henderson, George.** "Poor Southern Whites: A Neglected Urban Problem." *Journal of Secondary Education,* 41:111–114, March, 1966.

212. **Herndon, James.** *The Way it Spozed to be* (New York: Simon and Schuster, 1968). Metropolitan ghetto school in action.

213. **Hunt, J. M.** "How Children Develop Intellectually," *Children*, 11:83–91, May, 1964.

214. **Havighurst, R. J.** "Unrealized Potentials of Adolescents," *Bulletin of National Association of Secondary School Principals*, 50:75–114, May, 1966.

215. **Hewer, Vivian H.** "Are Tests Fair to College Students from Homes with Low Socio-Economic Status?" *Personnel and Guidance Journal*, 43:764–769, April, 1955.

216. **Iscoe, Ira** and **John Pierce-Jones.** "Divergent Thinking, Age and Intelligence in White and Negro Children," *Child Development*, 35:785–797, September, 1964.

217. **Jones, J. L.** "Assessing the Academic Achievement of Negro Students," *Clearing House*, 39:12–14, September, 1964.

218. **Katz, Irwin.** "Review of Evidence Relating to Effects of Desegregation on the Intellectual Performance of Negroes," *American Psychologist*, 19:381–399, June, 1964.

219. **Kohl, Herbert.** *36 Children* (New York: New American Library, 1967). An account of the author's experiences during two years as a sixth-grade teacher in a Harlem school.

220. **Kozol, Jonathan.** *Death at an Early Age: The Destruction of the Hearts and Minds of Negro Children in the Boston Public Schools* (Boston: Houghton-Mifflin, 1967).

221. **Kozol, Jonathan.** "Halls of Darkness: In the Ghetto Schools." *Harvard Educational Review*, 37:379–407, Summer 1967. Experiences teaching in the ghetto schools of a large American city.

222. **Loretan, Joseph O.** "Decline and Fall of Group Intelligence Testing," *Teachers' College Record*, 67:10–17, October, 1965.

223. **Loretan, Joseph O.** and **Shelley Umans.** *Teaching the Disadvantaged: New Curriculum Approaches* (New York: Teachers College Press, Columbia University, 1966).

224. **Mayerson, Charlotte Leon,** ed. *Two Blocks Apart: Juan Gonzales and Peter Quinn* (New York: Holt, 1965).

225. **Metz, F. E.** "Poverty, Early Language Deprivation and Learning Ability." *Elementary English,* 43:129–33, February, 1966.

226. [Mexican-Americans] *The Invisible Minority. Report of the N.E.A. Tucson Survey on the Teaching of Spanish to the Spanish-Speaking* (Washington: N.E.A., 1966).

227. [Mexican-American Education] Manuel, Herschel T. *Spanish Speaking Children of the Southwest.* (Austin: University of Texas Press, 1965).

228. [Mexican-American Education] "Viva La Raza: Mexican-American Education. A Search For Identity," *American Education* (Washington: Government Printing Office, 1968) (OE-38011)

229. **Miller, C. H.** "Counselors and the Culturally Different," *Teachers College Journal,* 37:212–217, March, 1966.

230. **Moore, John W.** *Mexican-Americans: Problems and Prospects* Madison, (Wisconsin: Institute For Research on Poverty, 1968).

231. **Morrill, Richard L.** "Negro Ghetto: Problems and Alternatives," *Geographical Review,* 55:339–61 July, 1965.

232. **Offenbacher, Deborah I.** "Cultures in Conflict: Home and School As Seen Through the Eyes of Lower-Class Students." *The Urban Review,* 2:2–8, May, 1968.

233. **Ornstein, A. C.** "Who are the Disadvantaged?," *Journal of Secondary Education,* 41:154–163, April, 1966.

234. **Pearl, A.** "As a Psychologist Sees Pressures on Disadvantaged Teen-Agers," *NEA Journal,* 54:18–19, February, 1965.

235. **Price, Kingsley.** "The Problem of the Culturally Deprived." *Teachers College Record,* 69:123–131, November, 1967.

236. **Radin, Norma.** "Some Impediments to the Education of Disadvantaged Children." *Children,* 15:170–176, September-October, 1968.

237. **Rainwater, Lee** and **William L. Yance.** *The Moynihan Report and the Politics of Controversy. Including the full Text of the Negro Family: The Case for National Action by Daniel Patrick Moynihan* (Cambridge: M.I.T. Press, 1967). Contains full text of the Moynihan Report and a discussion of its findings.

238. **Richey, E.** "Tenant Oppression: Our Smouldering Housing Scandal," *Antioch Review,* 24:337–50, Fall, 1964.

239. **Riessman, Frank.** *The Culturally Deprived Child* (New York: Harper, 1962).

240. **Rude, H. Neil** and **Donald C. King.** "Aptitude Levels in a Depressed Area," *Personnel and Guidance Journal,* 43:785–789, April, 1965.

241. **Savitsky, C.** "Social Theory Advances on the Disadvantaged," *High Points,* 43:785–789, April, 1965.

242. **Scales, Eldridge.** "Measured: What is the Standard?," *Clearing House,* 39:195–202, December, 1964.

243. **Schorr, Alvin L.** *Poor Kids: A Report on Children in Poverty* (New York: Basic Books, 1966).

244. **Schwebel, M.** "Learning and the Socially Deprived," *Personnel and Guidance Journal,* 43:646–53, March, 1965.

245. **Stalnaker, John M.** "Scholarship selection and Cultural Disadvantage," *Bulletin of National Association of Secondary School Principals,* (49:142–150, March, 1961).

246. **Warden, Sandra A.** *The Leftouts: Disadvantaged Children in Heterogeneous Schools* (New York: Holt, Rinehart & Winston, 1968).

247. **Webster, Staten W.** ed. *The Disadvantaged Learner: Knowing, Understanding, Educating* (San Francisco: Chandler, 1966).

TEACHING AND TEACHER EDUCATION

248. **Arnez, N. L.** "Effect of Teacher Attitudes on the Culturally Different," *School and Society*, 94:149–152, March 19, 1966.

249. **Arnez, N. L.** "Teacher Education for an Urban Environment," *Improving College and University Teaching*, 14:122–123, September, 1966.

250. **Bereiter, Carl** and **Siegfried Englemann.** *Teaching Disadvantaged Children in the Pre-School* (New York: Prentice-Hall, 1966).

251. **Bettelheim, B.** "Teaching the Disadvantaged," *NEA Journal*, 54:8–12, September, 1965.

252. **Bilingual Education.** *Hearings before the Special Subcommittee on Bilingual Education of the Committee on Labor and Public Welfare.* (U.S. Senate, 90th Congress, 1st session on S. 428, Parts 1–2, 1967). 2 vols.

253. **Bilingual Education Programs.** *Hearings before the General Subcommittee on Education of the Committee on Education and Labor.* (*House of Representatives*, 90th Congress, 1st session on H. R. 9840 and H.R. 10224, 1967).

254. **Blatt, B.** "Preparation of Special Education Personnel: Culturally Deprived," *Review of Educational Research*, 36:155–156, February, 1966.

255. **Brunson, F. Ward.** "Creative Teaching of the Culturally Disadvantaged," *Audio-Visual Instructor*, 10:30–32, January, 1965.

256. **Chamberlin, L. J.** "Teaching in the Large City," *Clearing House*, 39:483–486, April, 1965.

257. **Cordasco, F.** and **Charlotte Croman.** "The English Maiden and the Poverty Dragon: The Social Imperatives of Educational Change," *College English Association Critic*, 29:1–6, November, 1966.

258. **Cordasco, F.** and **Louis A. Romano.** "The Promethean Ethic: Higher Education and Social Imperatives," *Peabody Journal of Education*, 44:295–299, March, 1967.

259. **Cordasco, F.** "Teachers For Disadvantaged Youth: The City University of New York Program," *The New Campus*, 22:7–10, Spring, 1969; also in *Peabody Journal of Education*, 47:160–163, November 1969.

260. **Cordasco, F.** and **Eugene Bucchioni.** "An Institute for Preparing Teachers of Puerto Rican Students, *School & Society*, 100:308–309, Summer 1972.

261. **Cuban, Larry.** *Teaching In the Inner City* (New York: Macmillan Free Press, 1969).

262. **Eddy, Elizabeth M.** *Walk The White Line: A Profile of Urban Education* (New York: Doubleday, 1967).

263. "Evaluating Educational Programs: A Symposium," *Urban Review*, (February 1969), 3:4–26 [Includes an appended bibliography (pp. 27–31) on evaluating educational programs by Dorothy Christiansen.]

264. **Freedman, Philip** and **Nathan Kravetz.** "The Case of the Disadvantaged Teacher." *School & Society*, 96:204–205, March 30, 1968. Discussion of the urban teacher's dilemma in the education of the disadvantaged.

265. **Fuchs, Estelle.** "How Teachers Learn to Help Children Fail." *Trans-Action*, 5:45–49, September 1968. A case study of a new teacher in a New York City slum school.

266. **Haubrich, Vernon F.** "Culturally Disadvantaged and Teacher Education," *Reading Teacher*, 18:499–505, March, 1965.

267. **Kauffman, Joseph F.** "Responsibilities of Teacher Education Institutions for Expanding Educational Opportunities," in *Eighteenth Yearbook of American Association of Colleges for Teacher Education* (Washington: 1965). pp. 179–184.

268. **Koenigsberg, S. P.** "Teaching Disadvantaged Youth in Secondary School," *Journal of Secondary Education,* 41:17–24, January, 1966.

269. **Kozol, Jonathan.** *Death at an Early Age: The Destruction of the Hearts and Minds of Negro Children in the Boston Public Schools* (Boston: Houghton Mifflin, 1967).

270. **Levey, Seymour.** "Are We Driving Teachers Out of Ghetto Schools?," *American Education,* 3:2–4, May, 1967.

271. **Lewin, David.** "The Changing Role of the Urban Principal." *Elementary School Journal,* 68:329–333, April 1968.

272. **Lohman, J. D.** "Expose Don't Impose: Introducing Middle Class Values to Disadvantaged Children," *NEA Journal,* 55:74–6, January, 1966.

273. **McGeoch, Dorothy M.,** et al. *Learning to Teach in Urban Schools* (New York: Teachers College Press, Teachers College, Columbia University, 1965).

274. **MacKintosh, Helen K.; Lillian Gore;** and **Gertrude M. Lewis.** *Administration of Elementary School Programs for Disadvantaged Children.* Disadvantaged Children Series, no. 4. (Washington: U.S. Office of Education, 1966).

275. **Moore, G. Alexander.** *Realities of the Urban Classroom: Observations in Elementary Schools* (Garden City, New York: Anchor Books, 1967).

276. **Noar, Gertrude.** *Teaching the Disadvantaged* (Washington: National Education Association, Department of Classroom Teachers, 1967).

277. **Ornstein, A. C.** "Learning to Teach the Disadvantaged," *Journal of Secondary Education*, 41:206–213, May, 1966.

278. **Ornstein, A. C.** "Teacher Training for the Difficult School," *Peabody Journal of Education*, 41:235–237, January, 1964.

279. **Passow, A. Harry.** "Diminishing Teacher Prejudice." *New York State Education*, 55:6–10, February 1968.

280. "Preparation of Teachers for Depressed Urban Areas, Panel Discussion," in *Eighteenth Yearbook of American Association of Colleges for Teacher Education* (Washington: AACTE, 1965), pp. 111–125.

281. "A Proposal from Metropolitan College for a Summer Institute for Thirty Supervisors and Classroom Teachers of Disadvantaged Children in 1965," in *Eighteenth Yearbook of American Association of Colleges for Teacher Education* (Washington: AACTE, 1965), pp. 100–110.

282. **Rivlin, H. N.** "New Pattern for Urban Teacher Education," *Journal of Teacher Education*, 17:177–184, Summer, 1966.

283. **Rivlin, H. N.,** ed. "Teaching & Teacher Education for Urban Disadvantaged Schools," *Journal of Teacher Education*, 16:135–186, June, 1965.

284. School-University Teacher-Education Project. *Teachers for the Disadvantaged*; the report of the School-University Teachers-Education Project of the Research Council of the Great Cities Program for School Improvement in cooperation with Northwestern University. Edited and compiled by Michael D. Usdan, director, and Frederick Bertolaet (Chicago: Follett Publishing Company, 1966).

285. **Sciara, Frank J.** "Needed: Experienced Teachers for the Inner City." *Ohio Schools*, 45:24 ff., February 1967.

286. **Simon, S.** "Wanted New Education Professors for the Slums," *Teachers College Record*, 67:271–275, January, 1966.

287. **Stewart, Charles E.** "Racial issues Confronting Large City School Administrators." *Urban Education,* I:202–209, 1965. Guidelines that will help urban school administrators to assess the evolving nature of societal needs, ideals, and aspirations.

288. **Storen, Helen F.** "Making up the Deficit. Special Problems Facing Those Who Teach in Culturally Deprived Areas," *Clearing House,* 39:495–498, April, 1965.

289. **Strom, Robert D.** *The Inner-City Classroom: Teacher Behaviors* (Columbus, Ohio: C. E. Merrill, 1966).

290. **Strom, Robert D.** *Teaching in the Slum School* (Columbus, Ohio: C. E. Merrill, 1965).

291. **Syrkin, Marie.** "Don't Flunk the Middle-Class Teacher." *New York Times Magazine,* December 15, 1968, pp. 32 ff. Maintains that the true enemies of urban school children are "those who want to ghettoize education, and give unearned advances to the culturally deprived."

292. **Taba, Hilda.** *Teaching Strategies for the Culturally Disadvantaged* (Chicago: Rand McNally, 1966).

293. **Talbot, Alan R.** "Needed: A New Breed of School Superintendent." *Harper's Magazine,* 232:81 ff., February 1966. The difficulties involved in running an urban school system.

294. **Tiedt, Sidney W.,** ed. *Teaching the Disadvantaged Child* (New York: Oxford University Press, 1968).

295. **Tree, Christina.** "Grouping Pupils in New York City." *The Urban Review,* 3:8–15, September 1968. One of several articles in this special issue of *The Urban Review* concerned with the scope and the effects (on pupils) of teacher expectation in urban schools.

296. **Trubowitz, Sidney.** *A Handbook for Teaching in the Ghetto School,* (Chicago: Quadrangle Book, 1968).

297. **Tuckman, Bruce W.** and **John L. O'Brian,** eds. *Preparing to Teach the Disadvantaged: Approaches to Teacher Education,* (New York: Macmillan—The Free Press, 1969).

298. **U.S. Office of Education.** *Staffing for Better Schools Under Title I, Elementary and Secondary Education Act of 1965,* (Washington: U.S. Department of Health, Education and Welfare, Office of Education, 1967).

299. **Walberg, Herbert J.** and **Andrew T. Kopan,** eds. *Rethinking Urban Education: A Sourcebook of Contemporary Issues* (San Francisco: Jossey-Bass, 1972).

300. **Walker, Edith V.** "In-Service Training of Teachers to Work With The Disadvantaged," *Reading Teacher,* 18:493–498, March, 1965.

301. **Wayson, William W.** "Expressed Motives of Teachers in Slum Schools." *Urban Education,* I:223-238, 1965. Seeks to assess whether certain types of teachers would be more attracted to the deprived environment than would others.

302. **Willie, C. V.** "Anti-Social Behavior Among Disadvantaged Youth: Some Observations on Prevention for Teachers," *Journal of Negro Education,* 33:176–181, Spring, 1964.

303. **Wisniewski, Richard.** *New Teachers in Urban Schools* (Detroit: Wayne State University Press, 1968).

PROGRAMS AND MATERIALS

304. **Anderson, T.** "New Focus on the Bilingual Child," *Modern Language Journal,* 49:156–160, March, 1965.

305. **Anderson, V.** "Teaching English to Puerto Rican Pupils," *High Points,* 46:51–54, March, 1964.

306. **Antes, John M.** "Implications For the Elementary School of the Oberlin College Special Opportunities Program for Culturally Disadvantaged Children," *Childhood Education,* 43:370, February, 1967.

307. **Arnez, Nancy L.** and **Clara Anthony.** "Working with Disadvantaged Negro Youth in Urban Schools." *School and Society*, 96:202–204, March 30, 1968.

308. **Boykin, Arsene O.** "Measuring the Attractiveness of an Urban Elementary School." *Urban Education*, 1:39–45, Summer 1964. Concludes that "control of the attractiveness of an urban elementary school to experienced teachers is a matter of controlling the characteristics of the school and a matter of controlling the characteristics of its community as well as a matter of training teachers for 'difficult' schools."

309. **Bremer, John.** *The School Without Walls: Philadelphia's Parkway Program* (New York: Holt, Rinehart and Winston, 1971).

310. **Carlton, L.** and **R. H. Moore.** "Culturally Disadvantaged Children Can Be Helped: Self-Direction Dramatization in Reading," *NEA Journal*, 55:13–14, September, 1966.

311. **Carton, Aaron S.** "Poverty Programs, Civil Rights, and the American School," *School & Society*, 95:108, February 18, 1967.

312. **Clark, Kenneth B.** "Alternative Public School Systems." *Harvard Educational Review*, 38:100–113, Winter 1968. Discusses the obstacles to "effective, non-racially constrained" education, and proposes a strategy for providing excellent education in ghetto schools in conjunction with efforts to bring about effective school desegregation.

313. **Coin, H.** "English as a Second Language," *High Points*, 48:55–58, January, 1966.

314. Conference on Improving English Skills of Culturally Different Youth in Large Cities, Washington, D. C., 1962. *Improving English Skills of Culturally Different Youth in Large Cities.* (U.S. Office of Education. Bulletin 1964, no. 5, (Washington: U.S. Government Printing Office, 1964).

315. Conference on Teaching Children and Youth Who are Educationally Disadvantaged, Washington, D. C., 1962. *Programs for the Educationally Disadvantaged: A Report.* U.S. Office of Education. Bulletin 1963, no. 17, (Washington: U.S. Government Printing Office, 1963).

316. **Cordasco, Francesco.** "Urban Education—Leonard Covello and the Community School," *School & Society,* 98:298–299, Summer 1970. Benjamin Franklin High School in East Harlem, New York City.

317. **Crosby, Muriel.** *An Adventure in Human Relations* (Chicago: Follett Publishing Company, 1965). Report of a three-year project in Wilmington [Delaware] to curtail social blight and deterioratіηg conditions through the work of the schools with parents, children, and community.

318. **Dale, E.** "Vocabulary Development of the Underprivileged Child," *Elementary English,* 42:778–786, November, 1965.

319. **Dawson, Carrie B.** "A Cooperative Plan for Helping the Culturally Disadvantaged Reader," in Conference on Reading, University of Chicago, 1965. *Recent Developments in Reading . . .* (Chicago: University of Chicago Press, 1965), pp. 201–205.

320. **Derr, Richard L.** "Adaptive Strategies of Urban Schools," *Intellect (School & Society),* 101:88–90, November, 1972.

321. **Dillard, J. L.** "The English Teacher and the Language of the Newly Integrated Student." *Teachers College Record,* 69:115–120, January, 1968. The special language problem of the Black child in the integrated classroom, with stress on the need to teach standard English as a second language and to provide special drills in the beginning years so that later reading skills may be insured.

322. **Elkin, S. M.** "Minorities in Textbooks," *Teachers College Record,* 66:502–508, March, 1965.

323. **Elkins, Deborah.** "Instructional Guidelines for Teachers of the Disadvantaged," *Teachers College Record,* 70:593–597, April, 1969.

324. **Emans, Robert.** "What do Children in the Inner City Like to Read?" *Elementary School Journal,* 69:119–122, December 1968.

325. **Esser, G. H.** "Widening the Horizons of the Culturally Deprived," *ALA Bulletin,* 60:175–178, February, 1966.

326. **Fagan, Edward R.,** ed. *English and the Disadvantaged* (Scranton: International Textbook Co., 1967).

327. **Fantini, Mario D.** and **Gerald Weinstein.** *Toward a Contact Curriculum* (New York: Anti-Defamation League of B'nai B'rith). [1966]

328. **Fantini, Mario D.** and **Gerald Weinstein.** "Taking Advantage of the Disadvantaged." *Teachers College Record,* 69:103–114, November, 1967.

329. **Fantini, Mario** and **Gerald Weinstein.** *Making Urban Schools Work* (New York: Holt, Rinehart & Winston, 1968).

330. **Ferman, Louis A.,** ed. *Poverty in America: A Book of Readings* (Ann Arbor: University of Michigan Press, 1965).

331. **Frazier, Alexander,** ed. *Educating the Children of the Poor* (Washington, D.C.: Association for Supervision and Curriculum Development, NEA, 1968).

332. **Fries, Charles Carpenter.** *Teaching and Learning English as a Foreign Language* (Ann Arbor: University of Michigan Press, 1957).

333. **Furno, Orlando F.** and **Harry C. Hendrickson.** "Pupil mobility—Implications for Urban Education." *Urban Education,* 1:134–148, 1965. The effect of pupil mobility on urban school systems.

334. **Geltmen, Max.** "On Learning Swahili: Crisis in New York." *National Review,* 20:1160–1163, November 19, 1968.

335. **Giddings, M. G.** "Science Education and the Disadvantaged." *Science Education*, 50:206–212, April, 1966.

336. **Gittell, Marylin,** ed. *Educating an Urban Population* (Beverly Hills, California: Sage Publications, 1967).

337. **Gordon, Edmund W.** and **Doxey A. Wilkerson.** *Compensatory Education for the Disadvantaged: Programs and Practices—Preschool Through College* (Princeton: College Entrance Examination Board, 1966).

338. **Gray, Susan Walton.** *Before the First Grade: The Early Training Project for Culturally Disadvantaged Children* (New York: Teachers College Press, 1966).

339. **Harrington, Michael.** *The Other America: Poverty in the United States* (New York: Macmillan, 1962).

340. **Haubrich, Vernon F.** "Teachers and Resources in the Slum Complex," in *Claremont College Reading Conference. Yearbook.* Claremont, Calif., 28:40–50, 1964.

341. **Hillson, Maurie.** "The Nongraded School: An Organization For Meeting the Needs of Disadvantaged and Culturally Different Learners," *Hillson Letter #17: The Nongraded Elementary School.* (Chicago: Science Research Associates, 1967).

342. **Hillson, Maurie.** "The Reorganization of the Schools: Bringing About A Remission in the Problems Faced by Minority Children," (Phylon: *The Atlanta University Review of Race and Culture*), 28:230–245, 1967.

343. **Hillson, Maurie.** "Sociological, Psychological and Educational Correlates of Gradeless Schools," *Hillson Letter #3: The Nongraded Elementary School* (Chicago: Science Research Associates, 1966).

344. **Isenberg, Irwin,** ed. *The Drive Against Illiteracy* (New York: Wilson, 1964).

345. **John, Vera P.** and **Vivian M. Horner.** *Early Childhood Bilingual Education* (New York: Modern Language Association, 1971).

346. **Jones, W. Ron.** *Finding Community: A Guide to Community Research and Action* (Palo Alto, Calif.: James E. Freel, 1971).

347. **Klemm, Eugene.** "Appropriate School Programs," *Education*, 85:486–489, April, 1965.

348. **LaBrant, L.** "Broadening the Experiences of Deprived Readers," *Education*, 85:400–502, April, 1965.

349. **Lanning, Frank W.,** ed. *Basic Education for the Disadvantaged Adult: Theory and Practice* (Boston: Houghton Mifflin, 1966).

350. **Levine, Daniel U.** "The Community School in Contemporary Perspective." *Elementary School Journal*, 69:109–117, December 1968. The need for the urban school to function as a social institution involving the people of the neighborhood that it serves.

351. **Levy, M.** "Upward Bound: A Summer Romance?, "*Reporter*, 35:41–43, October 6, 1966.

352. **Lewis, H. P.** and **E. R. Lewis.** "Written Language Performance of Sixth-Grade Children of Low Socio-Economic Status from Bilingual and From Monolingual Backgrounds," *Journal of Experimental Education*, 33:237–242, Spring, 1965.

353. **Macauley, R. K. S.** "Vocabularly Problems for Spanish Learners," *English Language Teacher*, 20:131–136, January, 1966.

354. **MacCann, Donnarae** and **Gloria Woodard,** eds. *The Black American in Books for Children: Readings in Racism* (Metuchen, N.J.: Scarecrow Press, 1972).

355. **Metzner, Seymour.** "Classroom Tested Learning-games for Use in Urban Elementary Education." *Journal of Education*, 149:3–48, December 1966. The learning-game technique, and examples of games that have been successful.

356. **[Migrant Children]** *A Guide for Programs for the Education of Migrant Children* (Austin, Texas: Texas Education Agency, 1968).

357. [Migrant Children] *Guidelines For the Education of Migrant Children* (Sacramento, California: California State Department of Education, 1965).

358. Mingoia, Edwin M. "The Language Arts and Deprived Pupils," *Education*, 85:283–287, January, 1965.

359. Mintz, N. and H. Fremont. "Some Practical Ideas for Teaching Mathematics to Disadvantaged Children," *Arithmetic Teacher*, 12:258–260, April, 1965.

360. National Council of Teachers of English. Task Force on Teaching English to the Disadvantaged. *Language Programs for the Disadvantaged: The Report of the NCTE Task Force on Teaching English to the Disadvantaged* (Chicago: National Council of Teachers of English, 1965).

361. New Jersey Education Association. *The Disadvantaged Child: A Program for Action.* (Trenton, New Jersey: N.J.E.A.). [1965]

362. Niemeyer, John H. "The Bank Street Readers: Support for Movement Toward An Integrated Society," *Reading Teacher*, 18:542–551, April, 1965.

363. Olsen, James. "The Verbal Ability of the Culturally Different," *Reading Teacher*, 18:552–556, April, 1965.

364. Olsen, James. "Needed: A New Kind of School for the Slums." *Education Digest*, 33:4–7, January 1968.

365. Orem, R. Calvert, ed. *Montessori for the Disadvantaged: An Application of Montessori Educational Principles to the War on Poverty* (New York: Putnam, 1967).

366. Ornstein, Allan C. and Philip D. Vairo. *How to Teach Disadvantaged Youth* (New York: David McKay, 1969).

367. Passow, A. Harry, ed. *Developing Programs for the Educationally Disadvantaged* (New York: Teachers College Press, Teachers College, Columbia University, 1968).

368. **Passow, A. Harry.** *Reaching the Disadvantaged Learner* (New York: Teachers College Press, Teachers College, Columbia University, 1970).

369. **Perales, A. M.** "Audio-Lingual Approach and the Spanish-Speaking Student," *Hispania*, 48:99–102, March, 1965.

370. **Phelps, D. W.** "Project Headstart: A Professional Challenge," *Adult Leadership*, 15:41–42, June, 1966.

371. **Ponder, E. G.** "Understanding the Language of the Culturally Disadvantaged Child," *Elementary English*, 42:769–774, November, 1965.

372. "Poverty and Employment," *IRCD Bulletin*, 5:1–12, March, 1969. ["Strategies for Closing the Poverty Gap;" "Rich Man's Qualifications For Poor Man's Jobs."]

373. **Prator, C.** "English as a Second Language," *Bulletin of National Association of Secondary School Principals*, 48:113–120, February, 1964.

374. "Project Head Start," *NEA Journal*, 54:58–59, October, 1965.

375. **Reid, Robert D.** "Curricular Changes in Colleges and Universities for Negroes," *Journal of Higher Education*, 38:153–60, March, 1967.

376. **Riessman, Frank; Jerome Cohen;** and **Arthur Pearl,** eds. *Mental Health of the Poor; New Treatment Approaches for Low Income* People (New York: Free Press, 1964).

377. **Rogers, Donald W.** "Visual expression: A creative advantage of the disadvantaged." *The Gifted Child Quarterly*, 12:110–114, Summer, 1968.

378. **Rojas, P. M.** "Instructional Materials and Aids to Facilitate Teaching the Bilingual Child," *Modern Language Journal* 49:237–239, April, 1965.

379. **Ross, Frank E.** "For the Disadvantaged Student: A Program that Swings," *English Journal*, 54:280–283, 1965.

380. **Shaw, Frederick.** "Educating culturally deprived youth in urban centers," *Phi Delta Kappa*, 45:91–97, November 1963. An early study which traces the origins of the

problem of the disadvantaged, and shows how some large school systems confronted the issues.

381. **Smilansky, Sara.** *The Effects of Sociodramatic Play on Disadvantaged Pre-School Children* (New York: John Wiley & Sons, 1968).

382. **Smiley, M. B.** "Gateway English: Teaching English to Disadvantaged Students," *English Journal*, 54:265–274, April, 1965.

383. **Smith, L.** "Literature for the Negro Student," *High Points*, 47:15–26, October, 1965.

384. **Sowell, Thomas.** *Black Education: Myths and Tragedies* (New York: David McKay, 1972).

385. **Stroheker, Edwin C.,** ed. *If They Read: A Report of the Workshop in the Reading Problems of the Culturally Disadvantaged Child, July 12–13, 1965* (Louisville, Ky.: Department of Library Science, Catherine Spalding College, 1966). (Mimeo)

386. **Stull, E. G.** "Reading Materials for the Disadvantaged: From Yaki to Tlingit to Kotzebue," *Reading Teacher*, 17:522–527, April, 1964.

387. **Totten, W. Fred.** *The Power of Community Education* (Midland, Mich.: Pendall, 1970).

388. **Troupe, Carolyn H.** "The Whittier-Somerset Project: A Case Study in Urban-Suburban School Cooperation." *Elementary School Journal*, 69:123–128, December 1968. Successful experiment in bridging the gulf between urban and suburban schools.

389. **U.S. Office of Economic Opportunity.** Project Head Start. *An Invitation to Help Head Start Child Development Programs: A Community Action Program for Young Children* (Washington: Office of Economic Opportunity, 1965).

390. **U.S. Office of Education.** *A Chance for a Change: New School Programs for the Disadvantaged* (Washington: U. S. Government Printing Office, 1966).

391. **U.S. Office of Education.** *Guidelines: Special Programs for Educationally Deprived Children, Elementary and Secondary Education Act of 1965, Title I* (Washington: U. S. Department of Health. Education and Welfare, Office of Education, 1965).

392. **U.S. Office of Educational Research Information Center.** *Catalog of Selected Documents on the Disadvantaged* (Washington: U. S. Office of Education, 1966).

393. **Ward, Betty Arnett.** *Literacy and Basic Elementary Education for Adults: A Selected Annotated Bibliography* (Washington: U. S. Department of Health, Education and Welfare, Office of Education, 1961).

394. **Watt, Lois B.,** and others. *The Education of Disadvantaged Children: A Bibliography.* Educational Materials Center (Washington, D. C.: U. S. Office of Education, 1966). [Professional Resources; Elementary and Secondary School Textbooks; Children's Literature]

395. **Washington, B. B.** "Books to Make Them Proud," *NEA Journal,* 55:20–22, May, 1966.

396. **Wayson, William W.** "The Curriculum in the Inner City School." *Integrated Education,* VI:12–18, January–February 1968. The need for a more realistic curriculum for the inner city school.

397. **Wolf, Eleanor P.** and **Leo Wolf.** "Sociological Perspective on the Education of Culturally Deprived Children." *The School Review,* 70:373–387, Winter 1962. Maintaining proper perspective in considering the importance of socio-economic factors in learning.

398. **Wolk, E.** "Teaching English as a Second Language in the Elementary Schools of New York City," *Hispania,* 49:293–296, May, 1966.

399. **Wolk, E.** *A Summary Report of Reading Disabilities of Children Learning English as a Second Language.* Mimeo. (New York City; Board of education, 1963). A valuable report on early programs in behalf of Puerto Rican children.

400. **Yinger, J. M.** and **G. E. Simpson.** "Integration of Americans of Mexican, Puerto Rican and Oriental Descent," *The Annals*, 304: 124–131, March 1956. Notes various programs in New York City developed to maintain cultural pluralim.

401. **Zimmermann, Matilde J.** *Teachers' Guide For Afro-American History* (Albany: New York State Department of Social Services, 1969). Designed to help the non-specialist with the existing body of material on Afro-American studies and in establishing guidelines for evaluating new resources as they appear.

Index

INDEX

References are to entry numbers